Book Reviews: What Are ...g?

"Living with addiction is not a specta...it it or not we are affected. Well written, insightful and to the point, We Codependent Men, finally discusses the missing pieces for men whose lives are touched by addiction. Without a doubt I recommend this book for those men in need of healing and to those who love them".

Robert Ackerman, PhD, Chairman of Sociology Department, University of Pennsylvania.

"Finally! A book that gives a powerful voice to the quiet and hurtful truth of men whose lives are shattered by the addictions of those they love. A landmark book, **We Codependent Men,** plants the seeds of empowerment and provides real-life solutions for the enabler to reclaim his sanity. This must-read, life-changing book will catapult you from chaos to calm, and provide you with the valuable insights and tools you'll need to not just survive, but thrive! You'll want to revisit these pages again and again...."

J. CAROL PEREYRA, Editor in Chief , Going Bonkers Magazine

There is a need for this book for codependent men. In my association with the many men and women who attend 12 Step Retreats at Holy Name Passionist Retreat Center, the codependent men have the greatest fear and the least knowledge or understanding of their relationship with the addicted person in their life. As the man in the family, they are supposed to have the answers and they don't. This book begins to give some answers.

Fr. Joseph Moons, C.P., Retreat Director, Holy Name Retreat Center, Houston, Texas.

"You are not alone and there is help! For over 65 years, NCADD and our National Network of Affiliates have been on the front lines offering Hope, Help and Healing through education, information/referral, intervention and recovery support for millions of individuals and family members. And without question, NCADD has seen a dramatic increase in the number of men seeking help due to the alcoholism or drug addiction of a spouse, child or other family member. Without help, there are devastating consequences for everyone. And, thanks to Ken and Bob, "We Codependent Men" provides an invaluable resource specific to men and their unique recovery journey. Written from the heart of experience, the book provides powerful, inspirational personal stories and tools for recovery to serve as a guide and support".*

Robert J. Lindsey. M.Ed., CEAP, President/CEO, National Council on Alcoholism and Drug Dependence, Inc. (NCADD).

"Excited, Educated and Encouraged are the three words I would use to express how I feel about <u>We Codependent Men We Mute Coyotes.</u>

Excited: Never before has there been a book published that confronts this issue as thoroughly as this one. With all the books I have read over the years I have never come across a book that covers this life or death problem amongst men. Educated: After reading this incredible book I am more educated about my own codependency issues than ever before. I am now able to deal with them with a clear solution approach. Encouraged: Now more than ever thousands of men will be able to learn, apply and implement the solution and experience the freedom from codependency and pass it on to others who desperately need it.

You cannot miss this opportunity for a new life".

Monty D. Meyer, Executive Producer Take12Radio.com, KHLT Recovery Broadcasting

We Codependent Men We Mute Coyotes

Hope, Inspiration, and Healing
for Men Living with Addicted People

by Ken P., Bob T., and Carrie C-B.

RECOVERY

This book is dedicated to Michelle T. who died from the disease of addiction on December 24th, 2005. Spiritually she continues to live with her family and to help others who are suffering from this disease.

Preface

This book was written for the man who is living with an addicted person who still considers addiction a problem that he can solve on his own. If you are such a man, whether you have admitted it consciously or not; you see some loved-one's behavior as a problem that you may somehow solve. This misconception is not only perpetuating your loved one's disease; it is destroying you as well.

If you can read this book and learn about how addiction affects family members, then you have a chance for recovery. Your loved one's addiction is not a problem you can solve. You can only ask for help. As you will discover here, it is available from many sources.

*What we are saying is that you are absolutely powerless over someone else's addiction. You may be a CEO, a minister, a physician, an attorney, a policeman, a psychiatrist, or the president. Until you admit this fact first to God, to yourself, and to another human being, the true healing cannot truly begin. One fact that you may not realize is that you may be **part** of the problem! A clear way to see this problem is to use the following illustration: If you have planned a picnic and it has started raining, that is a fact. You cannot solve this fact. Your only choice is to decide how you are going to react to this fact. Once you understand that addiction is a fact, acceptance can follow. As you will read in our stories about how we tried to survive while living with addicted people, finally coming to that acceptance can be a horribly long and arduous process. May our book help your recovery process begin sooner.*

About the Authors

In keeping with 12 step recovery program tenants which state that "anonymity is the spiritual foundation of all our traditions," the three authors will not publicly disclose their names. However, they do wish to share how they have been impacted by the disease of addiction and how they have seen miracles bestowed in recovery within themselves and others.

The authors have at some point in time lived with addicted family members. Our stories include an alcoholic ex-wife, an alcoholic mother, an addicted daughter, and the affects of being raised in an emotionally abusive home. The third element to this book comes from the daughter of an alcoholic father and the ex-wife of a multiply addicted husband. Within this book are woven stories from fellow 12 Step members. These can be seen in quotes, stories and in various other aspects as a way to broaden the scope of co-dependency in men. No matter how you look at it chaos is chaos with varying *levels* in terms of the prices paid for the chaos by those who love someone with an addiction. Within our stories and the stories of others, you will see constant angst throughout decades with the most tragic story being the death of a daughter from a cocaine overdose. The authors and contributors battled this disease through control, raging, caretaking, and attempts at rescuing the loved one. The end results were problems that evolved into something more severe for everyone. Finally, the authors surrendered to a God or their Higher Power through Al-Anon or other 12 step programs.

Combined, the authors have been attending Al-Anon or other 12 step meetings two to three times a week for over 40 years. They have sponsored over 40 other 12 step program members. In addition to the meetings, the authors have collectively read various 12 step program literature, led and spoken at numerous meetings, and served on committees. As a result they have seen themselves and others change from complete despair, depression, financial ruin, and unbearable grief. The end result after surrendering and growing through 12-step programs were lives filled with serenity, joy, and freedom.

Table of Contents

Part Two: Coyote's Journey to Find Change

Part Three: Our Stories

Acknowledgements

There are so many who have contributed so much to this endeavor. First we must thank Scott B. who was with us at the very beginning of this project. We will be forever grateful for your contributions and insight.

We want to thank our family members who had to do without us while we worked to create this book. Jody, Marilyn, Melinda, Emily and Jax, thank you for your support and sacrifice. Bob L. and Loren G., your direct contributions to the manuscript strengthened it greatly. To Claire W., thank you for your careful guidance during the early stages of our writing. To the members of our local recovery community who spoke such honest words. Those words transformed into entries throughout the book we call "*heard at a meeting.*" Your collective love and wisdom sustains us every day. For those late night hours that Janet C. poured over design until she birthed and then polished our cover. Cary Lindsay whose knowledge of the publishing industry gave us such focused direction. We love you all and we owe you.

PART ONE:
THE LIFE OF THE COYOTE

Introduction: Why a Coyote?

We men who have lived with an active addict are no different than coyotes in the wild. We men are all secretive, furtive and cautious just like the coyote. As a result of these characteristics, there are always more of us around than most people realize. For example, there are so many coyotes throughout North America. They can be seen from all of Alaska throughout America all the way to the tip of Florida. Unlike their cousin the wolf which is considered an endangered species, coyotes are considered a nuisance. The rate at which these animals are killed is staggering, all because they fall victim to misunderstandings. Yet coyotes continue to expand their population and range. Coyotes are now a nuisance in places such as heavily populated downtown Los Angeles. As you read this book, you will come to realize that codependent men, like coyotes, are all around you every day. In fact, there is a good chance that **you** are one.

We codependent men, like coyotes, are survivors. We are scroungers. We are never finicky. If there is no meat available to the coyote, he will eat fruits and vegetables. If there is no game small enough to catch and overcome, he will become a scavenger and feed off of whatever is left after some larger carnivore has had its fill and left the scene. Codependent men are survivors and scroungers too. If there is no work available that is high paying and glamorous we will do menial tasks without a second thought. This makes us good providers in the workplace and highly successful in our careers. We fill such self-effacing positions as salesman, stocker or any servile service-oriented position involving assuaging the public.

This quality serves well in allowing us to fulfill our role as the primary enabler for an addicted loved one. For example: housework, washing clothes, chauffeuring the kids from one event to another; none of these duties are off limits for us. This makes a handy arrangement when we are strapped to addicted wives, mothers, and/or daughters. Their addictions render them so incapable and unwilling to do the "scud work" that a codependent man fits perfectly into the family picture. Put another way, codependent men and coyotes are alike in that they are both consummate "make doers". This is also one reason why the codependent man becomes a mute coyote. He is unable and often not even capable of speaking up for himself. He sells his services cheaply in a vain attempt to avoid the pain of conflict with his addicted loved one. In the end, he is as fully consumed by the addiction much like his loved one yet he may never take a drink, drug or hit from a substance. The scraps left behind by an addicted loved one becomes the food that feeds and sustains the codependent man.

At this point as a reader, you may be asking questions about several contradictions already described. Addiction and codependency are diseases that are said to be cunning and baffling by those of us engaged in recovery through 12-step programs. So how are all of these contradictions possible? For the coyote, how can we love our dogs of every imaginable size and shape, and yet hate this little wild coyote that we almost never see and who weighs no more than about thirty pounds? For the codependent man, how can we tolerate his obsequious fawning demeanor and continue promoting him up the corporate ladder until he is everybody's boss? Sometimes we hate the characteristics of others that we ourselves possess.

Imagine a codependent man and a coyote standing side by side. Neither of these creatures is a team player. Neither is loveable and cuddly. Both are self sufficient; neither asks for help. Both are taciturn, cautious and reserved. Both are also terribly capable and effective. Who wants to love a creature like that? Nobody does! But then, from the standpoint of the codependent man, we desperately *need* creatures like him in order to function smoothly in our complex social-cultural-economic systems. This is where the metaphor and title of this book derive: <u>We Co-dependent Men; We Mute Coyotes. Hope, Inspiration, and Healing for Men Living with Addicted People.</u>

Chapter 1: The Coyote and The Pack: Social Life

Coyotes are born into packs of 3-7 individuals, usually consisting of a mated pair and several pups of varying age. They are cared for carefully in the very early days after birth, even intimately. Older brothers and sisters help raise the newest pups and for the first three weeks the female nurses. Pups are generally born in liters of 4-6. After about three weeks of nursing, the other members of the family feed the babies by regurgitating partially digested meat into the pups' mouths. However, this pampering ends rather abruptly at about six weeks, after which each pup is totally weaned and basically left on its own to survive.

This early abandonment into harsh living conditions forces the pups to "grow up quickly". It also creates a situation that favors the famous "loner" personality of both the codependent man and the coyote. For example, unlike the domestic dog (which requires at least a full two years before it begins to act anything at all like an adult dog) the coyote, at one year, is usually separated from the family pack and surviving as a sole individual.

This "sink or swim" sort of childhood has created an animal that has for all of recorded human history been described as a creature that is "crafty". For hundreds of years, Native American story tellers have related colorful tales about coyotes, usually with a plot that involves what have been called "Trickster Tales."

Here is a first-hand experience of the husband of an addict. He was told a mythical tale about the coyote by a Native American while working on a corporate-government project in the Pacific Northwest.

"I have interacted for hours with modern day Native Americans in the Pacific Northwest and I was told one of these tales in Eureka California by a Hoopa Native American friend over beers; it was a great story complete with a moral message about the importance of humility. The story explained why "dog" (the Native Americans just call each animal character by their given name as though the individual in their story represents all dogs) has been loved and protected by man for so long, and coyote has had to fend for himself outside of the human camp. In the story I was told, coyote had been bragging that he could stay awake longer than they can, and so the Indians conducted a contest, with the one who could stay awake the longest getting to live in the Indian camp and the loser having to roam. In the end, coyote fell asleep and lost. The tale explained that the coyote to this day has a black scraggly tip to its tail because when it fell asleep next to the campfire, it didn't wake up until its tail caught fire, which made the story end with coyote having to endure both pain and embarrassment because of his bragging."

The story illustrates for the codependent male, his life is what is on fire. His life is full of silent pain and embarrassment due to the actions of the addicted loved one. Another way to look at how the coyote and codependent male coincide is to look at the cartoon character Wile E. Coyote. Fans have for decades laughed hysterically as this tragic-comic character who has tried every imaginable device to capture the roadrunner. Men, especially codependent men, can relate to this character on many different levels. We see ourselves in him, both as a protagonist and as an antagonist. We identify with his scheming but we laugh hardest when his scheming backfires and he becomes the victim. Wile E Coyote's spectacular failures strike us deep inside because we see ourselves so easily in him. When the writers cause the coyote excruciating pain and humiliation time and again, with one catastrophic unexpected outcome worse than the last, we howl with a mixture of sympathy, pain, and derision. The colorful cartoon coyote has a man's heart because the man *is* Wile E. Coyote in the flesh.

Like the coyote, the codependent man lives in a state of heightened diligence. He sees the other men as wolves running in their chosen packs. He sees the jocks, the golfers, the professional organizations, the fraternal clubs, the Little League Dads and the men in his neighborhood dressed in their crisp shorts. But the disease of addiction has isolated him. He has no pack for protection. For example, his preoccupation with an addicted wife has robbed him of the time and energy to form trusting relationships with other men. He pays a tremendous internal price for that missing element because somewhere down in his bones every man knows that isolation from the pack means death.

It is not only his lack of time to develop relationships with other men that isolates this codependent man; his various defense mechanisms such as perfectionism and over-achievement serve to make other men shun him. There is also his underlying anger, mostly born of fear. Other men sense this anger. He is so obviously not at ease in his own skin. He over-reacts; especially to any criticism. Therefore, his ears are either perked in constant high alert or flattened with anger and frustration. His frustration cannot be voiced because he cannot identify exactly what is keeping him from speaking. The word he is looking for is called *denial*. His most immediate and user-friendly shock absorber against the painful blows delivered at random from first his dysfunctional family of origin and then from his addicted fam-

ily member. This becomes his greatest barrier to finding relief. This changes the codependent man into something he never imagined.
He becomes a mute coyote.

He must remain silent like a mute coyote. Coyotes remain silent lest they draw attention to themselves.

Heard at a meeting: "I tend to run between no boundary at all and the Berlin Wall!"

Attention, to a man married to an addicted family member, is synonymous with pain. The act of avoidance of pain has gradually become his moment to moment purpose in his life. His tail is ever between his legs as though he is trying to make himself smaller. The wagging of his puppy hood spiked tail filled with high expectation has been replaced because a wagging spiked tail would destroy the "cover" that he has inadvertently created over the years.

The process of becoming a mute coyote is one that evolves with time and various situations. The evolution does not happen all at once. The process is groomed over time and becomes a silent partner in the male's life. For example, when drug researchers want to induce stress ulcers in mice, the most efficient test model involves using a cage constructed so that the mice cannot avoid putting their feet on the bottom of the cage. The bottom, however, delivers a painful electric shock. The mouse **has** to touch the bottom and he knows he **will** be shocked but there is absolutely no way that the mouse can anticipate **when** the shock will occur. The shock is initiated by a computer set for random delivery. It is not the pain of the shock that induces the stress ulcers so quickly in the test subject. It is the mouse's **anticipation** of the pain. Like the mouse in the experiment, the codependent man knows that the pain will come and that it will hurt in the very ways that stress him most. He just does not know when the pain will come because the actions of an addict are random and at times unpredictable. The codependent male will be embarrassed, ridiculed and demeaned through the actions of the addict. The anticipation of those actions is the driving force behind the codependent man's emotions. He learns that by staying silent he minimizes pain. However, he also knows deep down that the pain will eventually come; no matter how hard he tries to be mute.

The Birth of the Mute Coyote: Place within the Pack

Coyotes are the only canine capable of what psychologist's term "observational learning."

Although observational learning can take place at any time during an organism's life cycle it assumes special significance during the organism's early months or years. Therefore, another factor favoring this capacity lies in both the coyote's and the codependent man's early maturation process. Unlike dogs and wolves, the coyote takes on a full adult role after less than one year after birth vs. two years for other canines. Coyotes, like codependent men, tend to experience a shortened childhood. We assume adult responsibilities earlier than most other creatures. Dovetailing with this early maturity is the tendency to be raised by fathers who were for one reason or another not emotionally available or absent altogether. Men raised by fathers who themselves experienced the Great Depression and World War II are prime early adapters. Also, men whose fathers died early in their childhood or were workaholics, or traveled a great deal or divorced their mothers while they were pregnant tend to grow up to be "little Dads."

Heard at a meeting: "My father was the highest power in my family"

Codependent Man's Life as a Cub

We will begin at the beginning of the codependent disease process as it relates to childhood with some concepts long accepted among 12 step program people. The process begins with the roles typically played by children in dysfunctional homes. What follows will answer the question most often asked of professionals when they work with the families of addicted loved-ones, "But how did this happen to our family?" We owe a huge debt of gratitude to Sharon Wegscheider; whose work Another Chance first described these roles in 1981. There have been many courageous writers, who led all three of us to our insights but by far the most influential has been Melody Beattie, whose works are not just present in our home libraries; they are worn, torn, dog-eared and annotated after years of re-reading. The following section of this chapter is provided as a brief summarization of our understanding to describe predictable roles of children from addictive homes through the writings of Sharon Wegscheider and Melody Beattie.

The **Class/Family Clown** draws attention away from the pain and dysfunction at home by entertaining others. This child is "cute." He or she is always truly immature but plays up the immaturity to draw attention away from the big people who are the dangerous dysfunctional addicts. Inside this child is filled mostly with insecurity. The following quote from the work From Survival to Recovery describes this child beautifully.

> "To diffuse the battles that often raged around us or to divert our parents from their attacks on one another or other members of the family, some of us learned to entertain. We tried to blunt family crises with jokes, stories, musical performances or even comedy revues. We became quite talented and popular with our classmates. Society rewarded us with the laughter, applause and attention but in time we found that even when we desperately wanted to shed it, the mask would not come off. We felt driven to perform and talk compulsively even when we were exhausted or needed comfort ourselves. Intimacy was difficult for us to achieve because tender or passionate

moments prompted us to joke or wisecrack." (Survival, P.15)

The **Scapegoat Child** acts out; gets into trouble and gains attention while deflecting attention away from the addicted parents. This child is constantly in trouble. There is open defiance of authority with anger the favorite escape. This child is most likely to sport an outrageous personal appearance utilizing whatever is currently 'in' at the time in social circles. At the beginning of the 21st century this typically includes various body piercing, tattoos, the so-called "gothic" look or maybe brightly colored spiked hair. This child will also (at any cost) defy the family to the point where schooling is affected and may even become suspended, expelled, or drop out altogether. The ultimate goal of this child is to do the direct opposite of any authority figure.

The **Hero Child** is the child who fantasizes that if he or she accomplishes enough, then the whole family will be "Ok" and look "normal" to the outside world. This child is overly conscientious; conforms to all rules from authority and constantly strives for approval and acceptance from everyone, especially adults. In spite of being a high achiever, the hero child always feels inadequate. This child will also be the member of the family who will try to make sure harmony is present within the family at the cost of his/her own emotional needs.

The **Super Enabler** is the child often closest to the addict emotionally. This child is the family 'workhorse'. Typically if a daughter, this child assumes the household chores left undone by both the addict and the codependent parent. If a son, this child is constantly trying to protect his mother if the addict is his father. Either way, inside he or she typically has low self-esteem and there is much unexpressed anger. The favorite fantasy and role is that of the martyr and this child is the one most likely to be presented to members of the medical profession because another favorite attention-getting device for the super enabler is hypochondria.

The **Disappearing Child** is typically played by children in addicted households. To avoid the pain of the chaos and conflict in the living room, which seems to be where most of the drama occurs, the disappearing child finds predictable ways of escaping.   One way is to adopt another family altogether. This is often another family on the same block where the child has formed a trusting friendship with a playmate and that playmate's family has created a welcoming safe home. Throughout childhood this home is where the disappearing child heads right after school after checking in with Mom, Dad or an older sibling. Here is where the disappearing child "hangs out"; where snack foods and meals; TV, easy banter and acceptance are always available in endless supply. The disadvantage (or possible advantage) of this escape is the loss of closeness with others in the nuclear family. The advantage, besides avoiding dysfunction, may be life-long friendships formed and maintained with these really special neighbors; unless of course the process is interrupted by a family crisis or constant moves by the nuclear family. This phenomenon of constantly relocating or "the geographical cure" will be explored more fully in another chapter.

Another escape for the disappearing child is to retreat to his or her room. Here solitary hobbies like building models or playing dolls are favorites. Modern kids plant themselves in front of the computer playing video games or escape with TV. Another solitary favorite is reading. Reading as an escape mechanism is often demonstrated by either or both parents and of course, the school system routinely rewards students with the uppermost reading abilities, so there is reinforcement for reading throughout childhood. Therefore, this becomes the easiest escape or behavior of the disappearing child.

One disadvantage for reading, along with the other solitary activities, is weight gain. Every generation before this one assumed that childhood would include thousands of hours spent out of doors engaging in sports and games that were active. Inactivity juxtaposed with constant snacking on convenience foods results in obesity. We needn't belabor the magnitude of the obesity problem among our children but looking deeper into the stone, current all-time high rates of addiction among parents cannot help but contribute to this national crisis.

Finally, there is the ultimate disappearing act...the one that happens deep inside the imagination. Here children retreat to whatever world they can conger; often complete with imaginary playmates. Taken to extreme this can lead to psychosis. This is seen most evidently in the electronic media with which we all must react if we are living in one of the developed countries during the twenty-first century encourages both inactivity and isolation. Drive through neighborhoods throughout America after school and count the number of children out-of-doors playing with other children. Chances are there are significantly fewer than what most of us experienced in our own childhood. This is where the disappearing child literally removes him or herself away from any outside human contact ever becoming more isolated from reality. This is due in part to the fact that the true reality in which this child lives is extreme and often unbearable.

Life within the Pack

Once the roles within the child are set, they can translate into the daily family life.

This can include the addict and the codependent second parent or any combination of step-parents and step children. These roles can be seen within both divorced and intact families.

The most common role exhibited by children is that of the **hero**. This is natural because the hero child is (more often than not) the first child born into the family. This child was schooled from birth to fix an unhealthy relationship. As the first-born, this child was always treated as special by everybody in the family because he or she was the first on the scene among many adults. Only one can be the first-born. This child routinely receives more attention, praise, handling, instruction and just plain love than children born later. He or she is also usually perceived as "ahead" of the younger children, simply because that is the truth. This child is also more likely to assume a helping parent role with subsequent children and is probably well ensconced into this role by the time later children are born. Later children simply come onto the scene. These children cannot possibly compete with this older, physically larger sibling and fall into other roles that are not taken.

Typically, the second child becomes the *scapegoat* but in time, especially if a third child is born, the **disappearing** child role, or the middle child role is commonly assumed. The youngest child in larger families finds the class/family **clown** role a natural because he or she is little, cute and enjoys this status conferred by not only the parents but the older siblings.

So it is no accident that first-born children most often adopt the hero child role and this is even evidenced in their selection of professions. For example, the helping professions are disproportionately represented among these people. Hero children fit well as ministers, physicians, nurses, teachers, social workers, police officers and especially as *therapists!*

The Human Pack: Real Life with an Addict and Codependent

It requires four reasonably functioning people to maintain a single nonfunctioning addict. These four are forced to practice a unique sharing of the lies that form the spider web supporting the addict. They are usually the immediate members of the addict's family.

First, there has to be one primary enabler. For addicted women, for example, this is typically a high functioning husband, a wealthy father or a boss who spreads the work the addict doesn't do among many other workers. In time these dysfunctional enablers are sucked into the addiction vortex because addiction is a disease that is *progressive.* That is, it creeps into systems slowly over many years. As the addict gradually declines in functional capacity, others in terribly subtle ways take up the slack.

Maybe in the early days the addict wife's husband will cover for her by doing routine chores. He prepares more meals, washes more clothes or stands in as the only parent during back-to-school night. Here is the husband taking his kids to the pediatrician or playing with them at the park while mom is at home throwing up or less dramatically, she's "…just too tired." An example of such a scenario would begin like this:

"You guys just go ahead and go. I have to stay home with this headache."

The reasons for the headache are as diverse as the alcoholic's imagination but whenever she manages to shift her guilt to anybody else (usually her husband and/or kids) she makes them responsible instead of her alcoholism. The terms are accepted by the family members.

The husband hears her bad mood like this;

"She is mad at me because of the fight we had last night when I said that awful thing about her mother."

The oldest daughter (who is probably in the super-enabler role) might interpret this as;

"Mom is upset this morning because I didn't do enough of the housework yesterday."

Little brother (who might be in the disappearing child or class/ family clown role) might translate;

"Mommy is mad because I wet the bed again last night and she has to stay home to wash the sheets."

The missing link behind their response is that the family members are not at fault for the actions of their addicted loved one. Their lady of the house has functioned for months now without feeling good.

She hurts inside...physically, mentally, emotionally and spiritually. She lives in a world parallel to that of her husband where the single goal of each moment is to minimize pain. But, for her part, she has the added burden of minimizing the pain while planning every event to coincide with her need for the security she knows only the bottle can provide.

In order to fully understand the process of minimizing pain, we will draw a quote from Caroline Knapp's best-selling book, <u>Drinking, a Love Story.</u> (25)

> *"The need is more than merely physical; it's psychic and visceral and multi-layered. There's a dark fear to the feeling of wanting that wine, that vodka, that bourbon; a hungry abiding fear of being without;, being exposed without your armor. In (AA) meetings you often hear people say that, by definition an addict is someone who seeks physical solutions to emotional or spiritual problems. I suppose that's an intellectual way of describing that brand of fear and the instinctive response that accompanies it. There's a sense of deep need and the response is a "grabbiness"; a compulsion to latch onto something outside of yourself in order to assuage some deep discomfort."(p. 58)*

So the whole family is in the tight grip of the lady's deep need for alcohol or drugs. That is why modern terms deem it "a family disease". The great lie; the great secret kept by everybody is that the lady of the house is an addict. The issue is beyond a moral question; beyond shame. It is an absolute. It is a fact manifested through refusal by everyone in the family to be willing to admit this truth deep within them. This refusal perpetuates everybody's pain therefore being carried from generation to generation.

Both partners in the addiction dance are highly subject to what retailers call POP (or point of purchase) in advertising which leads to financial implosion. This dynamic involves a momentary feeling of happiness that comes when some eye-appealing object is seen on the store shelf and immediately purchased. This can be seen in ways such as having frequent garage sales every month because so much junk was purchased over the years. It was always just "stuff" like books, bobbles and beads that did in no way help the financial situation. Eventually you learned to check yourself by asking every time you started to buy some new toy, "how much will I get for this in the next garage sale?" Empty fulfillment cripples the dynamics within the relationship because the feeling the stuff evokes is only temporary but sadly this realization may come too late. When this evolves into making major purchases such as cars it can lead to a common outcome with addiction...bankruptcy. This effect can be best summed up by the following reality: "You are broke all of the time because you keep buying things you don't need with money you don't have trying to impress people you don't know!"

Moving the Pack; the Geographical Cure.

For various reasons, the members of addicted families suffer constant upheaval from frequent relocations. Moving may be related to other obvious symptoms of family instability; bankruptcy, divorce, frequent hospitalization, incarceration, deaths in the family, etc.

But there may be other reasons. The former hero-child of an addicted mother who is now a father is more likely than most dads to sacrifice family stability in order to climb one more rung up the corporate ladder. Even more often, when the marriage starts to disintegrate one or both parents may try the "geographical cure."

Here is how it goes:

"...maybe we can just start over in Arizona,"

or

"...I'll take that promotion in the home office so that the extra money will take the pressure off of us"

or

"...besides, everything has to get a lot better when we move

closer to her family...her Mom will straighten her out once and for all!"

There are at least three flaws in the geographical cure solution to addiction. First, each move breaks the bonds just beginning to form where the family currently lives. There is real glue holding together healthy families after spending years forming supportive relationships with neighbors, family, and friends. When this bonding is severed, further issues arise such as those dealing with trust and a sense of security. Also, built-in support systems like boy scouts or girl scouts, relationships with teachers, school, and church gain in value with *time*. If those support systems are removed from the child then instability will occur leading to other issues later in life.

Secondly, even among the members of healthy families, a move is stressful. The strain imposed by having to adapt to new schools, neighbors and regions has been well documented. Issues surrounding trust are some of the key factors that influence how the child will function with each move. A key life skill is diminished in the fact that the child is not able to build upon relationships (which can hinder future relationships as an adult) furthering the cycle of dysfunction over time.

The final and most significant factor stressing the family members in a geographical cure is always the disease of addiction itself. Everybody who moves brings themselves along for the ride. Dad still has his overachievement/control issues; little brother still wets the bed and big sister is still trying to match wills with Mom. She has her teenager hormonal imbalance and mom has the unpredictable mood swings of any alcoholic. Therefore, geographically things are different but the issues at hand still lurk and now have a whole new set of problems attached – the problem of constant change.

Here are the unspoken rules in a dysfunctional household:

1. *People always love with strings attached.*
2. *Reward comes only from performance.*
3. *You are not a human being; you are a human "doing".*

4. *There is always emotional instability; that is reality.*
5. *Never show your true feelings. That can result in punishment, ridicule or abandonment.*
6. *Always take on more responsibility than you can handle; this is heroic.*
7. *Using evasion and half truths to cover up the truth about the way your family lives is not only necessary; it is noble.*
8. *Conformity is rewarded.*

The one cardinal rule in all of these dysfunctional roles is the rule that *nobody ever criticizes any alcoholic in the family*. No child wants or has the authority to view his parents, uncles, aunts or grandparents as "bad" or inadequate. This sets up a system based on denial and lies. The unpredictability of the emotional states of the alcoholic adults around him creates a constant low level of anxiety in the child. There are no absolute truths. What was true three minutes ago is not true now. This is the life of the cub within a dysfunctional pack.

Heard at a meeting: "We had no mole hills in the house where I grew up; just mountains."

Chapter 2: Survival of the Coyote: Codependency

The coyote is an "opportunist." He eats anything he can catch and is an omnivore in every sense of the word. Like raccoon and bears, coyotes are omnivores. Coyotes will take fruit; anything alive they can catch and overcome and, if hungry enough, even carrion left by other predators.

Codependency is now well described as a personality type by mental health professionals. The following three types of codependency are presented so that the reader can understand the characteristics of the codependent, as well as better identify behaviors associated with each type of codependency. Do not be surprised if you read some characteristics here that closely fit somebody you know or love or if these codependent types may fit you.

Codependent Type 1: Super Enabler

The basic distinguishing characteristic of all the members in the addicted household is denial. Therefore, the super-denier codependent is the type who has simply perfected denial. These people adopt every excuse made by the addict and assimilate it into their main functionality daily. They blame anybody else for the consequences inevitably suffered by the addict. They even make up their own excuses. This kind of codependent supports their addict financially and a major portion of time and energy is spent cleaning up every mess the addict makes. For example, in the role of a parent of an addict, when one divorce after another happens to their addict son or daughter this type of codependent parent will always blame the failure of the latest marriage on the latest marriage partner. The super-denier codependent is most obvious when there is a situation with elderly parents with an addicted child but this situation is certainly not exclusive to the age of the parent or the age of the child. You might have a single son in his thirties or even forties with two high functioning parents who have a surplus of money. The situation might resemble the following:

"Yes, Robby has just been left by his third wife but she was never right for him anyway. Her mother never liked Robby. Her mother drove a wedge between Robby and his wife…his drinking was never the problem."

Notice that these doting parents still call their adult son by his childhood name and they still support him; not only financially but emotionally. He calls his mother every day. One or both of his parents' daily existence still revolves around him. He gives them purpose. He also gives them commiseration and status from neighbors and other family members. It might be seen by members of the parent's social circle as follows:

"Henry and Cynthia are just wonderful people for taking care of that pitiful Robby after all of these years." If this couple doesn't get help with their codependency and finally allow their "child" to suffer the consequences of his or her behavior they will literally love their Robby to death."

Heard at a meeting: "I no longer have to be my son's airbag."

How far can this denial be taken? For instance: take a certain codependent man whose soon-to-be ex-wife continued charging on his credit cards while he continued paying the monthly bill. Sometimes the addict wife was spending this money while dating other men. His denial was so strong that he just could not *believe* that money was the only thing left that she wanted from him. Also, his denial would not let him accept that the marriage was really over. In some of these situations, when he cancels the credit cards she suddenly has a change of heart and grants him the divorce he has been seeking after months of delay. Incidentally, with the changes in roles that have happened during the past few decades this scenario is often reversed with the high functioning codependent wife continuing to maintain a high-paying professional career while supporting a philandering addicted husband. Therefore in all actuality, codependency is not exclusive to men but in men it is mostly silent. It is a part of becoming a mute coyote.

Codependent Type 2: In Charge

The second type of enabler actually needs the flaws of the alcoholic or addict that keep their loved one being irresponsible so that they can stay in control. What better set-up for this passive-aggressive type than to have a respected, outwardly dominant spouse (for example) who is indebted and guilt-ridden because of the years of misbehavior. This codependent man remains poised to remind himself of embarrassing situations from decades ago as a means of maintaining control. The "good one" makes all of the real adult decisions in the family. An addicted woman, for example, with this kind of an enabler at home is not a spouse so much as she is a hostage. This situation can be especially debilitating to the addict because the controller secretly does not want recovery for fear of losing their power position. If the addicted woman ever hits a bottom and goes for help, the codependent in charge will need to contact his fellow 12 Step program supporters in order to survive.

The high functioning husband with an addicted wife in this situation gets pay-offs left and right from his wife's negative behavior. He is in control of the family and he simultaneously enjoys admiration from everybody outside the family living room because he appears to be such a saint when compared to his wife's offensiveness. The wife's addiction is a double payoff for him. If a geographical cure of moving the family is in place, neighbors quickly start talking when this new family moves into their area. Right away the co-dependent in charge starts taking care of other people's yards; watching over their property when they travel and chatting with them socially. In the meantime, sooner or later, somebody on the block will have an exchange with his wife and it will not be so pleasant. The talk that starts around the block sounds similar to this;

"He is a wonderful guy; I just love him but he has to be a saint to put up with that wife of his."

Codependent Type 3: Non-Existent Person

The third type of codependent is the most pitiful. This person needs somebody else in the scapegoat-blustering-abusive role in order to be complete. This codependent thinks so little of himself that he only *exists* as a reflection of the other person. This person could be compared to a spider on the mirror. If the addict is the spider and the codependent only the reflection of the spider in the mirror then the reflection has opted out of making any life decisions. The reflection just reacts to every move of the spider never taking the risk involved in making personal choices or decisions. The dependency is so complete here that, should the spider walk off of the mirror, the reflection disappears. Given those dire consequences, the name of the game for the non-existent codependent is doing everything necessary to avoid being abandoned. There is just no limit to which the reflection will go to accommodate the behavior of the addict. Public humiliation at the hands of the addict is by far the most common consequence faced by the non-existent codependent.

This role is often favored by many women living with an addicted man. It has been observed for decades that a woman is much more likely to stay with an addicted husband or wealthy addict father for financial and security reasons than is a man of an addicted wife or mother. Most men will leave the addict wife usually to go and find another woman that he can dominate; most codependent women will stay with an addicted man as long as he continues functioning well enough to support the family. This is why her bottom so often comes when he loses his last job. For everyone there is a different bottom…a different "last straw"; be it infidelity, loss of health, domestic violence, incarceration, or bankruptcy for the codependent (whose very identity depends upon the addict) that bottom is likely to be a very low one.

Because these behaviors developed over a long period of time it is not reasonable to expect them to disappear overnight. Detaching from our closest family members is the most difficult detachment of all. We love these people and they love us. These are the people who cared for us when we were helpless; who loved us when we were not so lovable. They gave birth to us or married us and bore our children. We shared Christmases, birthdays, paychecks and colds with them. We changed their diapers. However, even in the face of all of this history, we can only recover from our sick dependencies upon them when we do the hard work of changing ourselves from the inside out.

Most truths come to us through other people such as parents, teachers and preachers. Other truths, however, come to us from personal experience and those are always the most profound. One truth that is most evident after you have gone through the recovery process is this: you never harm another person by growing yourself. You are half of every relationship so when you grow you make the sum of the relationship greater. Some will just not grow with you. Some are not willing to do so; some do not know where to start and some never even think that thought. There are many ways to make the break from family members in order to grow. Some have to sever the relationship altogether for a period of time. Some can continue the relationship on a shallow level and then allow the depth to come another day. Some have to accept the fact that the other person is never going to change. These are hard truths. The good news that comes to us through recovery is that change is possible. Change in thinking, change in behavior, change in attitude...all of this awaits the recovering individual who is willing to put forth the time and energy necessary to effect that change.

Coyote in Training:
How to Train a Man to Become an Enabler

If he somehow overcomes all of the stumbling blocks mentioned so far the codependent man has one more hurdle to overcome and this one can be the most difficult of all. He has been trained. The codependent man has been trained by his addicted loved-one's disease to accommodate this person's need for the drug in thousands of subtle ways. Here is how this works. Biologists have distinct classifications of animal behavior on a continuum from instinct to critical reasoning. Just above instinct is a process called "habituation." Habituation is a sort of non-behavior. It means that some stimulus in the animal's environment results in neither reward nor punishment so it is ignored. As an example, if you take a horse out of the pasture and put it under a police officer in a major city that horse is suddenly exposed to an entirely foreign environment. The first time an irate driver blasts a horn that animal will be startled. However, after a period of habituation, the horse ignores all horn blasts.

Husband's Perspective on Enabling

Habituation comes into play with a codependent married to an addict. The constant angry looks; the general air of depression throughout the home; the smells and sounds of the addiction (i.e., how distinctive is the sound of a beer can opening?)...all of these stimuli eventually become habituated and ignored. There is the problem. What is the solution?

With time, God and the program; an adult man raised as a hero child can learn to trust somebody other than himself. After going through the fourth and fifth steps (see chapter eight in the recovery section) the responsibility for the chaos that the codependent man really deserves is teased out from that over which he was truly powerless since he was a little kid. His inventory includes his positive qualities as well. The patience, capacity to nourish other people, and hard work ethic that he formed as devices to survive are all still there. The anger, fear, caretaking, worry, lying, over-achieving and shame are all well on their way to being discarded because they have been identified. Eventually there is growth to the point of being able to forgive. The years of resentment bottled up in the hero child have blocked his contact with himself, with others and, most tragically, with God.

Father's Perspective on Enabling

Early in our Al Anon and Nar-Anon recovery programs we hear about the concept of enabling behavior. This is usually defined as doing things for the addicted loved one to prevent them from experiencing a laundry list of consequences that occur because of their addiction. The result of this behavior is that the addict's self esteem is damaged and their desire for recovery diminished. They also come to resent us and we in turn become frustrated, angry and resentful because our "help" almost always makes the situation worse. While this definition makes sense to us, we find later that it is extremely difficult for us to recognize our own enabling behaviors and even more difficult to stop them. This is especially true for parents of addicted children.

The father of an addicted daughter, for example, faces a gut wrenching dilemma when he must accept that he can no longer protect and make things OK for his little girl. This dilemma goes right to the core of a father's basic instincts and his perceived role as a man. After numerous failures to "help" his daughter he typically takes on an equally powerful motivator to continue to "help". This motivator is guilt and is the result of thinking that he is a failure as a father and as a man. He finds many justifications for continuing to "help" including thinking that this time it will work and that, as a father and a man, he simply must continue to try to do something. Taking some kind of action also provides temporary relief from the pain of watching his daughter suffer. So how does he get out of this dilemma?

The single most important thing is to accept that his daughter has a disease over which he has absolutely no control or power. This acceptance must occur in his mind, heart and soul or he will be pulled back to the instinctive protective mode. Once the acceptance has occurred, he can move on to the next step which is separating his daughter from her disease. He learns that he can love his daughter but hate the disease. This distinction then allows him to discern what is enabling versus what is helping and loving. Often by this time he has lost sight of the beautiful person his daughter is and becomes focused entirely on her behavior. It can be helpful to think about and write a letter about his daughter's good qualities and even more helpful to both he and his daughter to give her this letter.

Woman's Perspective on Enabling

Why is it that to the outside world enabling looks like someone who gives the addict money when they are unable to pay their bills? In fact enabling is so much more than money related that we become blind to how it has infected our daily living. An addict feeds off every little thing or action that is given to him or her to the point where consumption of those little things becomes a part of the addiction that fuels it without any chemical consumption.

Enabling is the "little things". Enabling means little things such as doing the laundry for the addict when he or she is passed out so that they can to go to work without stains on their clothes because we need the additional income. Enabling means little things such as making the next day's lunch so that the addict won't be so stressed in the morning or because making the lunch lessens the feeling of guilt due to the fight earlier in the day. Enabling means little things such as taking the addict's car to get the oil changed because the light has been on in the car for weeks.

Enabling can become big things such as paying all the bills because the addict is not responsible enough to remember when the bills are due and the budget is too tight to afford overdraft charges. Enabling means: self-appointing ourselves as the head of the household to ensure that all the normal duties in maintaining a family flow go smoothly as seen by the outside eyes of our neighbors. All the while on the inside the walls are rotting and our lives are on a fast flying train to a destination of serial mental breakdowns. Enabling means being consumed by the disease of addiction without any mind/body altering chemical entering our bodies to render us addicted. *Yet enabling itself can become an addiction because our lives are unmanageable unless we manage someone else's life.* We become self-appointed life managers of our addict loved one.

The Tail Tucked Coyote: Physical Effects of Codependency

After being removed from the pack, the coyote is left to fend for himself. Scouring the plains for food and shelter his physical appearance begins to decline. He becomes thin and shaggy due to loss of sleep and constant movement. Coyotes and codependent men are what military drill instructors term "hard asses." They are tight and tough. They often literally cannot have a normal bowel movement. Seriously, the most common ailment of all animals capable of observational learning is constipation. In codependents, this translates into a whole constellation of ailments of the lower gastrointestinal tract, including irritable bowel syndrome (IBS), hemorrhoids and diverticulitis, etc. The upper gastrointestinal does not fare well either;

as problems with digestion are so closely related to emotional stress. Stress ulcers, especially duodenal ulcers in men, are the "wound stripe" of the codependent male. Hiatus hernia resulting in some-times pathological "heartburn" (or the now popular term, GERD, for gastro-esophageal reflux disease) keeps these men chewing antacid tablets and drinking Maalox directly from the bottle sometimes day and night.

Stress does untold damage to every human organ system. The gastrointestinal tract, the immune system, cardiovascular system, and respiratory system; it is these body systems that bear the brunt of the effects. To make matters worse, in their attempts to deal with the stress, codependent men turn to all manner of self-destructive habits such as drug and alcohol abuse themselves, smoking, and too often "comfort eating" which leads to a constellation of ailments centered on obesity.

One of the most common comments heard from codependents living with addicted loved-ones is *"I never know which personality will walk through the door."* This creates a situation with constant ambivalent feelings for the codependent. Recent clinical studies have actually identified this as a source of long-term health risk for the codependent. Unpredictability from a loved-one is actually more stressful than living with somebody you genuinely dislike. As a way to illustrate this seemingly contradictory effect, Drs. Holt and Lundstad at Brigham Young University address that very topic. Below are the results of their study.

"If you need another excuse for getting out of a fractured friend-ship, here it is: Stressful friendships may be bad for your heart.

A new study published in the Annals of Behavioral Medicine (June 25, 2007) suggests that the stress of unpredictable love-hate relationships, characterized by ambivalence, can lead to elevations in blood pressure...

"The type of friend we are talking about is someone we may

really love or care about," said Brigham Young University psychology professor Dr. Julianne Holt-Lunstad in a press release. "However, they can also at times be unreliable, competitive, critical or frustrating. Most people have at least a few friends, family members or co-workers that fit the bill."

In a previous study, the psychologist found that blood pressure is even higher around friends for whom we have mixed feelings than around people we clearly dislike. Holt-Lundstad and her collaborators at the University of Utah estimated that as many as half the relationships in an individual's typical social network could be categorized as ambivalent.

So for reasons of the heart----you might consider finding ways to spend more time with friends with whom you can relax and making extra efforts to let go of toxic friends. "The important point is that cardiovascular disease develops slowly over time, taking decades to develop," said Holt-Lunstad. "If such blood pressure increases are a pervasive part of your everyday life, your risk would go up."

"Most of the research out there has focused on the positive aspects of relationships and in fact indicates that social relationships are beneficial psychologically and physically," Holt-Lunstad said. "However, not all relationships are positive and some relationships may actually be sources of stress."

Husband's Perspective on Physical Affects

Having sponsored over 30 men during the past 30 years, I can anecdotally list the most common complaints I heard from these men. The complaints include constant colds, flu, sinusitis and other respiratory ailments; along with constant lower gastrointestinal problems associated with constipation, hemorrhoids and spastic colon. Another result has been psychological ailments associated with chronic depression.

The following ten physical ailments are taken from the web site *Alcoholism and Marriage* and are generally considered physical ailments experienced by women who are married to alcoholic husbands. Yet for the codependent male these aliments are often experienced by married men with an addicted wife. In general, the following list would also be experienced by any person who is constantly exposed to high levels of stress.

1. Depression
2. Heart Disease
3. Fibromyalgia
4. Chronic Fatigue Syndrome
5. Chronic sinusitis
6. Unexplained joint pain, night sweats, or fever.
7. Excessive weight gain or loss
8. Migraine
9. Chronic fatigue and immune deficiency syndrome
10. Spastic colon or IBS (Irritable Bowel Syndrome)

Heard at a meeting: "When you go up against alcoholism you don't just lose; you are a loser."

Woman's Perspective on Physical Effects

Physical effects of living with an addicted person were becoming a normal occurrence in my life. If it was not constant headaches, it was strep throat or at its worst, MRSA staph infections that lead to hospitalizations. Each time like clockwork, the addict in my life would relapse or move deeper into addiction, I would become extremely ill. This creates a really difficult place for the codependent loved one because we feel that sickness for us is not an option. Therefore, we do not take care of our illness fully which leads to a recurrence of the illness with even more ferocity. It becomes painfully apparent that stress not only clogs up our minds and actions but can tear down our bodies.

We forget that in order to help our families or addicted love one, we must first attend to our very own needs. Failure to do so can lead you down a road your body wishes not to go and that can yield not only death in the mortal sense but death in the mind. This becomes a place that is consumed by darkness. It becomes a place that if you are not physically well, you will never be able to claw your way out of with clarity and strength.

How the Coyote Feels: Walls and Stuffing

For most men, coping skills for the vast feelings in living with an addicted person are something that is void because of the lack of emotional management. This lack of skills for dealing with the vast emotions leads to anger with the end result being the stuffing or avoidance of feelings altogether. In order to understand this concept, one must first look at some of the common emotions expressed when there is an addicted individual in his life. Men are analytical in general; therefore problem solving skills related to emotions are foreign. In the culture given to men in the early developmental years, emotions are irrational and void of logic. This is where the male cannot apply those concrete problem solving skills so readily used in other aspects of his life when faced with emotional situations where the logic is not even in the equation. When dealing with an addicted person, the male begins a process that spins out of control and can lead to various other dysfunctions in his life as a result of his misunderstanding of the feelings occurring in his daily life. To identify those feelings is the step in the right direction to learning coping skills along with emotional management.

The initial feeling is anger which most commonly is the direct result of depression. The interpretation made by the codependent male is that the situation of addiction in his life is the direct result of his inability to be a "real" man or control the addicted person by applying reasonable, rational objectives. Rationality does not even compute in the complicated array of addiction. When the desired result is not achieved through analytical thinking, impulsiveness enters the cycle. This impulsiveness becomes the action taken by the codependent male in association with the emotion of anger and depression. The codependent male may commit adultery; become excessive in spending or fall into something else that creates an even more complicated situation. Impulsiveness is the direct result of a lack of the skills necessary to evaluate or manage emotions. In a sense, impulsiveness and codependency are one and the same because addiction itself is the result of one's inability to control the urge or the impulse to use drugs or alcohol. Codependency is a form of addiction with the difference being that no mind altering substance has been introduced into the body. A codependent male may choose to not become addicted to a substance and at times become defiant toward addiction. The result is an impulsive effect or action based on the actions of the addicted loved one. For some men, this becomes his addiction. The addiction for the codependent is an addiction to anger that manifests itself in very aspect of his daily life.

The opposite of impulsiveness can also occur as well if a male does not have a current addicted person in his life. He may have lived with someone as a child who was addicted or his parents may have lived with someone who was an addict. His emotional problem solving yields a different approach that presents itself as more of a personality problem. Thoughts can include the impression that life is harsh and filled with gloom or he may come across as arrogant or at worst he may become the absent father or husband. The cycle continues into the next generation where the son or daughter tries to fill those voids caused by the absent father who lacked the skills to problem-solve his emotions that began in childhood as a result of addiction by a loved one. The father appears distant and the children then interpret that in a way which he or she views an addictive substance as a way to fill the void immediately. This is where the cycle of failure in emotional skills management by the codependent begins and spins continuously until he seeks help from a 12 step program.

A 12 step program aids in the building of skills necessary for emotional management through association with others who are functioning and practicing those coping skills while living in the world of addiction. This is where the coyote needs a pack. This pack is more than a group of fellow sufferers; it is a unit comprised of answers on "how" to change behaviors in the individual coyote while helping him identify his strengths in his coping skills as well as point out areas for improvement. The result is a change in patterns that changes the direction of the cycle of addiction.

Father's Perspective on Feelings

Codependent men are not like codependent women. Men and women are just different. For codependent women there is often a need to set boundaries and to learn how to maintain them. For codependent men there is more often a need to lower walls.

Walls are safe places for a man who has been around alcoholics or has been married to an alcoholic wife. The reason why silence is so preferable to opening up and exchanging words is because *words are how alcoholics most often inflict pain*. The walls that build in time around the inner parts of a man render him more and more stagnant. The word stagnant means "not moving, or stale." Water is a lot like spirit. Spirit that is not moving, like still water, becomes stagnant. Stagnant water and stagnant spirit stinks...maybe that is why an oral tradition in Al-Anon is to call this 'stinkin' thinking!' Lowering the walls that held in the stinking thoughts is a different process for a man. There are thoughts like resentment for hurtful words uttered by a drunk. There are thoughts like self pity that we love to resort to because self pity allows us to feel like there is SOME sort of payoff. Those walls, when they are lowered, allow us to drain the inner swamp of the stuff that stinks!

In the beginning, when the time comes we often lower a wall on one side of our inner swamp with our first sponsor and he allows the stinking dark thoughts to just dissipate away into the universe. Then we start going to meetings and we listen. We listen a lot. That listening starts to bring in fresh water. At last there are fresh thoughts. We read our literature and that brings in more cool fresh water...new cleaner, clearer thoughts.

Finally, we lower two more walls...the two most important walls of all. The first is the inner ring of walls that blocks us off from our own feelings. There is a tiny compressed densely packed residue of true feelings inside most men. This is all that is left after we have stuffed our feelings year after year. That wall has become like a tough seed coat around a pinto bean. Beans have to be soaked...sometimes for a long time, before they can take in water. Our beans have to be soaked in the spirit of the program. The softening of that hard seed coat is the toughest job a man will ever do in his life. To be honest, after sponsoring many men through the years, I have had to accept the fact that many men are simply not able to do that softening! But if they do; inside every seed coat is an embryo. The embryo is new life that, once freed, can now begin stretching its roots into the moist nutrient rich soil of the Al-Anon program. Our new roots start pulling up rich stuff like wisdom and laughter...nutrients that we forgot we ever had...and just plain old love.

Husband's Perspective on Feelings

All she said was "You need to replace those air filters in the hall." My stomach instantly knotted. Furious thoughts answered in my thoughts. How can she order me around? I'm not some little kid she can boss. I have credentials. I teach higher math and science and have won awards for achievements in industry. Who in the hell does she think she is?

Thank God there is enough maturity from years of program to know when to keep my mouth shut and just keep moving until I can figure out what is going on inside. The adult me is arguing with some little kid me like this; "all she did was say out loud what has been niggling you about doing all week. Why are you reacting so strongly? You really don't want to say these things you are thinking to the woman you love more than life itself, do you? How much would it hurt her if you blurted out all of this fury?"

We are all feeling creatures; whether we want to admit that or not. For men this is almost like an admission of fault. Repression is the process where thoughts, memories and feelings are pushed downward someplace in that vast organ we call the brain. Psychologists call this place the unconscious. Without getting too technical, let's just say that they go to a place so far removed from our moment-to-moment thought processes that they no longer disturb us. In the case of really, REALLY painful feelings, this is not always something bad. What addictionologists term "denial" is a handy and effective emotional shock absorber. Here is the rub; repression does NOT mean that painful feelings no longer affect our thinking.

When we men have painful feelings we simply stuff them, so they are never processed in a healthy or timely fashion. With the word "timely" I mean right now; as they happen. We simply deny them to ourselves. We are so adept at this that we do it without a second thought. However, feelings that are denied are not feelings that are gone forever. These repressed feelings remain dormant and hidden until triggered by some modern every day event. When this occurs they re-surface but, because they have been hidden for so long, we do not ourselves know their origin. We just know that suddenly we are over reacting to some normally insignificant event.

The following morning, after "sleeping on it," I realized what had happened. As a child I worked with my Dad building houses. Every day, while we were working, Dad would first yell my name from someplace in the house and then order me to help him hold something, or assign me to "...get out there and clean that lumber."

I was a little guy. Dad hit and he hit hard with his belt. There were no options and any defiance...even a LOOK, resulted in huge pain preceded, accompanied and followed with verbal abuse. When my wife called my name from another room and then told me something that needed to be done, years of stuffed fear and anger came from way down there and my twelve year old boy felt it all at once."

Heard at a meeting: "Feelings have no right or wrong."

Woman's Perspective on Feelings

It is thought in some realms that feelings and women are synonymous. Therefore one cannot exist without the other. Addiction takes away feelings and replaces them with more descriptive words than mad, angry, crying, sad and the plethora of other simple terms for feelings. Addiction turns those simple words for feelings into monstrous words such as anxiety, depression, mania, hostility, irrationality and a deluge of other large words that originate single word; resentment. The entire collage of feeling words (large or small) is ultimately the offspring of pure resentment. As loved ones of an addict we resent the fact our birthdays are forgotten; the bills were not paid when it was the addicts turn; the embarrassment of the stagger and yellow eyes of our addict loved one around our friends and family or the shear annoyance in a simple household assistance request left unacknowledged. All of these actions (or lack thereof) renders us helpless to the feelings we wish not to allow because we are self-deemed mighty home holders who are to keep the world afloat while our addict ventures through life in a self-induced numbing fog.

Feelings are not simple. The only simple thing about feelings regardless of whether you are male or female is that they are not rational and can never be defined or linked in a clear fashion to one single event. They are a conglomeration of years of feelings coupled with controllable and non-controllable events associated with those who we love, work with, or choose as friends. Feelings are not created overnight; they build beautifully or fester boisterously and leave us to veil them in order to protect our own bruised egos that are left in the shadows of addiction.

The Coyote in Fear:
How the Codependent Male Becomes Scared

Heard at a meeting: "I can be calm but still feel the feelings."

One of the last feelings associated with stuffing in the coyote is that of fear. Fear comes from anger at the addicted one by way of frustration, hurt, disappointment and so on. In this fear arena, codependency fully emerges. Below are 3 most common fears of a co-dependent:

1. Fear the word will get out that their loved one is an addict.
2. Fear you will be left alone to pick up all the pieces left so selfishly behind by the addict.
3. Fear you are a part of the addict's problem and every action you do causes the addict to continue in the addiction.

It is not being said that these are the exact fears for every codependent, but they are very real and do in fact become a part of the codependent's coping skills used to manage emotions. This type of ill fated thinking overrides the codependent's ability to identify the feelings; feel those feelings and find solutions. It generates the following acronym commonly used in 12 step programs: ***Fear is False Evidence Appearing Real***. Fear is nothing more than a lie we tell ourselves without the help of a 12 step program. That program is designed to see those faults associated with fear; draw them to the surface; find ways to move forward; all while knowing you are completely supported by a group of people who have been in the exact position you live in at that moment. It becomes a moment that will be seen as a way to change and as a way to manage the emotional side of addiction.

The Coyote Becomes Addicted:
Common Addictions for Codependent Men

Addictive substances and behaviors work. They provide temporary relief for intense physical, emotional, mental, and spiritual agony.

We codependents have our own favorite addictions.

To most of us the word addiction brings to mind images of down and out souls whose lives are lost to drugs and alcohol. That group actually represents only a fraction of the population whose lives are hampered by addiction. If we must do the numbers, it is generally accepted that only about 3% of the population is in the "down and out" state usually associated with hard-core addicts. Recovery litera-ture is just now starting to identify the "high-bottom drunk" only the correct terminology at the turn of the millennium is "high functioning alcoholic." (See New York Times Best Seller Drinking; A Love Story by Caroline Knapp and An Uncommon Drunk by Dr. Jeff Herten).

If you are a purest and you include all addictive behaviors; almost no citizen is exempt from the label. The list below is taken from the book Serenity. A Companion for Twelve Step Recovery. (

17)

"Addictive agents are those persons or things on which we form an excessive dependency."

1. *Alcohol or drugs*
2. *Work, achievement and success.*
3. *Money addictions, such as overspending, gambling, hoarding.*
4. *Control addictions; especially if they surface in personal, family, and business relationships*
5. *Food addictions*
6. *Sexual addictions*
7. *Approval dependency (the need to please people)*
8. *Rescuing patterns toward other persons*

9. *Dependency on toxic relationships (relationships that are damaging and hurtful).*

10. *Physical illness (hypochondria)*

11. *Exercise and physical conditioning*

12. *Cosmetics, clothes, cosmetic surgery, trying to look good on the outside*

13. *Academic pursuits and excessive intellectualizing*

14. *Religiosity or religious legalism (preoccupation with the form and the rules and regulations of religion; rather than benefiting from the real spiritual message).*

15. *General perfectionism*

16. *Cleaning and avoiding contamination and other obsessive-compulsive symptoms.*

17. *Organizing, structuring (the need to always have everything in its place).*

18. *Materialism*

If you are a relatively healthy person physically, emotionally, and mentally, you will list about eight of these. If you are a codependent, you might suffer from some or all of the above.

Woman's Perspective on Addictions

In the counseling profession we have a term called co-morbid. That term evokes shivers because it sounds like death. Death is what it becomes for someone living with an addict because not only do we have an addict of substance abuse in our lives but another person who is addicted to codependency; **US**. Not only was I addicted to codependency but to controlling everything in my immediate environment. Control was my co-morbid addiction. When the substance abuse was active and in our home, organization was the escape for me much like alcohol and prescription drugs were for the addict. The amount and intensity of organization on my part ebbed and flowed much like the addict. The intensity to which the feelings were ignored or left un-validated; the faster the label maker went to work. This feeling of control would fester and grow. It would show itself in the moving of items to make it easier for the addict to find things since the state of mind for the addict was always blurred and he would lose track of where things belonged in the house. I thought if I planned for the worst and had everything in its place then when the sky would fall I would be ready. I found myself absorbed in organizing and controlling my physical environment much like the addict does in their addiction. The result was that many of the responsibilities I had self-appointed due to my enabling, began to slip; leading to even more anxiety. My life became out of control because I could not control that which I could not see – myself; the codependent. This is the cycle that addiction can have on someone and they can never take a drink; a hit of joint; pop a prescription pill or inject a needle. The out of control train of addiction is addiction no matter the vice which makes it run.

*Heard at a meeting "I've heard the expression "gut feeling" translated as **G**od's **U**rgent **T**elegram."*

Chapter 3: Coyote's Manhood: Admitting Powerlessness

The constant state of fear imposed on the codependent man, if it is associated with the women in his life from the beginning, sometimes leads to men who turn anger toward all women. This is especially true for men raised by alcoholic mothers (and Scott B. will address that in detail) but for men married to alcoholic women there is always a great deal of anger. In exactly the same way that the women in Al-Anon sometimes enjoy engaging in "man-bashing" sessions, the male 12 step programmer finds it easier to blame all women for the pain inflicted by his alcoholic wife's disease.

Male Coyotes Differ from Female Coyotes

The reality of the culture in America today is that men are *treated* differently than women. Starting in early childhood we are taught the value of self-sufficiency. Throughout our childhoods we are told in millions of subtle and not-so-subtle ways that we are to be "big boys."

One aside needs to happen here. There is a profound generational distinction that needs to be made. Men born before about 1950 have *much* greater difficulty surrendering to the diseases of alcoholism and addiction. We were raised by fathers who knew first-hand the experiences of the Great Depression and WWII. These men lived through circumstances that forced them to mature to self-sufficiency very early and therefore they had little sympathy for "cry-babies." A man does not do the following: cry; complain; ask for help; admit defeat or quit...ever.

Al-Anon, a 12-step program offering support for the families of alcoholics, is based on the assumption at the outset that no person has the power to stop an alcoholic from drinking. This *powerlessness* is so absolutely the opposite of our upbringing as men that very few men can *ever* unlearn their early training and admit it. In taking the first step in any 12 step program, a male coyote has reached a bottom that leaves him completely vulnerable and sends him into a learning curve that is foreign and at the very least uncomfortable. The mute coyote is raw, exposed, torn, and desperate to find relief therefore the first step becomes a saving grace that lifts the weight of the world off his shoulders.

The first step says;
"We admitted that we were powerless over alcohol and that our lives had become unmanageable."

Men cannot imagine that they even belong in a 12 step program. As it states in the opening pages of Al-Anon's great book From Survival to Recovery:

"His isolation and confusion about the significance of his terrible loss at the very start of life are among the common characteristics all of us share who have grown up in families affected by alcoholism."

While men react by controlling, raging and taking action; women tend to try to be better wives or mothers; do more for the addict and redouble their efforts to use nurturing to solve the problem. Given these differences in how men and women feel, think and react when confronted with addiction, it follows that men also approach recovery differently than women. Also, men are different from women in many respects beyond their use of language and this is especially true in how they react when faced with someone else's addiction. This book is intended to provide help specifically for men and to fill a gap in recovery literature which is for the most part written by and for women. For example, the two male authors experienced frustration when attempting to find recovery literature and meetings that focus on how men think, feel and react to the disease of addiction. We have also heard many other men, both new and experienced in the recovery process, express this same frustration.

Most men do not know what they are feeling and when they do, anger is usually the only feeling that is expressed. In addition, unlike women, they are not willing to share feelings in any setting much less in front of a group of 12 step program women. Almost all the literature available on recovery for people living with addiction is written by women. As a result, men usually do not connect with the principles of a 12 step program when they first encounter them at a meeting or in reading the available literature. They first need to be able to relate to a man who is or has been in their situation and learn they are not alone in how they feel and react to the disease of addiction.

If you are a man reading this who suspects that you have a person addicted to anything...alcohol, drugs (hallucinogens, opiates, marijuana, or prescription drugs) food, sex, work...or shopping, please get some help. It's out there

Father's Perspective on Powerlessness

Men just think and act differently when confronted with addiction. They are driven to take action immediately rather than to talk about the problem with others as women generally do first. When repeated attempts to fix the problem fail men become angry and frustrated thinking they are a failure. They also become confused because what has worked in the past to solve problems does not work when dealing with addiction. Men are consummate problem solvers at their workplace...they have to be in order to succeed. After repeated failures to "solve" the "problem" of addiction guilt sets in and they become even more motivated to "solve the problem." I once heard this cycle described as what happens when a big bear picks up a burning hot garbage can; gets burned; gets madder and therefore squeezes harder!

Husband's Perspective on Powerlessness

God showed me this principle one Tuesday when I attended two Al-Anon meetings in one day. I slipped out of the Medical Center where I was working and attended a noon meeting at a church. It was a typical meeting for that day (the late 70's)...about 25 women and me. I shared during the meeting and as we all walked across the parking lot to the nearby cafeteria for lunch a woman made it a point to walk up beside me. She just sort of "lit into me" in an accusatory tone but what she said was "...You're the only man I ever heard who made any sense. All other men just want one thing and they are not even capable of thinking about anybody else." That night I met a man I was sponsoring, and he began right away unloading his own brand of disgust for the opposite sex. "Women only want two things from a man...a dick and a meal ticket!" Since that night I have viewed alcoholism as a disease. It is a disease of all human beings and neither sex has a monopoly on the misery.

In sponsoring many men during the years I can tell you that codependent men have tried everything imaginable to "manage" an alcoholic wife. They spent sometimes hundreds of thousands of dollars on treatment centers; begged and pleaded; sought out countless counselors; called the police and hauled their wives to the offices of one physician after another as their wives' bodies deteriorated from the inexorably slow physical and mental decline caused by swallowing alcohol. Admitting powerlessness was not an option for these men. If you are such a man, please get yourself to an Al-Anon meeting. We guarantee you that growing in self control, spiritual depth, selflessness and character will not render you less manly.

What if Your Wife Is Having An Affair With Alcohol?

After having sponsored over 30 men through the years in Al-Anon I can speak with some authority about the universality of certain frustrations these men experience. One such frustration always involves their having to deal with constant need for sexual release. An addict will leverage any advantage to perpetuate his or her addiction. In a situation involving an alcoholic wife the granting or withholding of sex translates into "final word" power which she uses to easily control her enabling codependent husband. Besides, in a very real way, the alcoholic wife is having a torrid affair with what she considers the true love of her life...her alcohol.

Last Sunday our minister delivered a powerful sermon on the topic of "Marriage: How do I live to honor and cherish?" He described the three kinds of love as *Eros* (romantic or sexual love), *philos* (brotherly or sisterly love) and *agape* (totally unselfish love involving commitment and sacrifice for another). As I sat there in the pew I thought about what happens to a marriage when one partner loves their addictive substance more than the other partner in their marriage. That love leaves no time, interest, energy or passion for *any* other entity. Is sex and romance possible? How can that be with somebody who has drugged themselves into near oblivion? Are brotherly and sisterly love even possible? How can that be when there is the total absence of even the awareness that another human exists? Is sacrifice for another possible? Is there any person on earth more self-centered than an alcoholic? Almost every man I ever sponsored eventually parroted back to me the same words I heard from my own first wife to rationalize her self-destructiveness: "...What do you care? It's my body, not yours. I can do whatever I want with it."

What a loss. Yes, addiction destroys the body, the mind and the soul of the addict. But it also destroys that fantastically beautiful entity called a marriage. As for the other half...the half left deprived of every form of love possible between a man and a woman, that loss will forever remain untold.

Woman's Perspective on Powerlessness

To know power is to have experienced power. As the addict consumes the drug of choice, they feel the power in which their bodies and minds change to the state in which they feel life is manageable. Yet as we all know once they have consumed the substance so enters the Jekyll and/or Hide affect. This is where we as the loved one of an addict begin the reactionary process called power. We attempt to control every aspect of the addict's life to the point to where we are searching the home for the colorful pallet of bottles filled with liquid or the amber colored smaller cousin with white lids with a label present or absent in the hope of concealing its identity. We want power over the addict, our children, our boss, our employees, and over the person in front of us in the car who cannot drive according to our standards.

Control means "no control" with the attempt to force something to fit into what we see as the right way of living. A force that literally takes us away from our present lives and leaves us festering in the past or constantly planning for the sky to fall and everyone will know what goes on inside your home. It is control over the outside images everyone sees only to leave a beast inside ourselves to control us. All the dreams, hopes and expectations we thought our addict loved one could fulfill are left dangling from a lifeline filled with booze or prescription drugs. This is where we exercise our control over someone who can never meet the minimum standards put in place by us because we have not ourselves accepted the fact that we as codependents are unequivocally powerless over addiction. In order to gain pure power we must give up power because power cannot be controlled and someone else, such as God, is the only one in control.

Heard at a meeting: "I was like a dog hanging onto someone's leg. I wasn't going to let go until they admitted that I was right!

Chapter 4: Coyote Has Feelings: Shame, Guilt, Self-Pity, Hitting Bottom

A common ploy of the addicted individual is bluster. There are various ways to gain respect. The most difficult is to use the personal discipline to grow first on an individual basis (by maturing in areas such as self control, patience, etc.) and then to go out and lead a fruitful life. Another way is to intimidate, fight and bluster at other people. This method makes the incorrect basic assumption that respect and fear are synonymous. Unfortunately, addiction is progressive. That is, it starts at a seemingly innocent level and then slowly grows until it takes the addicted person's everything; including their body, mind, soul, bank account, relationships, career...and respect. Psychologists studying the members of families suffering from addiction cannot pinpoint the exact point when true respect is replaced by false bluster but they know that it eventually happens. The addicted person has to become a bully because he or she senses the loss of their genuine respect from others (and even themselves) in time to their disease. Unfortunately, the other members of the family, being human beings themselves, respond to the abusive bluster in various predictable ways.

Codependent man, upon awakening.

"Hun, after sleeping on what you said last night during our

argument, I realized that you were right. I was totally wrong about that issue, and I want you to know that from here on out I'm going to change my ways. The most important person in my life is you, and I don't want to do or say anything that would make you unhappy."

Addict wife.
"Oh yeah?" Well I changed my mind."

A common response for a man is to answer in kind. How many times have we encountered terribly successful men in their careers who go home and react like irresponsible teenage boys when forced to interact with an abusive addicted teenaged child or wife? He may be the beloved senior manager at the office but, like Rodney Dangerfield, he "gets no respect" at home! The children witness the disrespect shown by the addicted wife, for example, and then they begin losing respect for both parents. In order to survive, since loud profane abusive behavior seems to work so well for the parents, the children sometimes join in the fray. At this point, the family members are no longer members of a family. They each devolve into an individual organism trying his or her best to survive in a threatening environment. We have many tools through recovery to reverse this downward spiral but none of us is strong enough to reverse what took years to develop. We need the daily support of others who have experienced recovery.

Son's Perspective on Shame and Guilt

Honesty is a requirement of Al Anon. I had always considered myself an honest person however as I progressed in Al Anon my understanding of honesty changed as well. I had to be honest about everything in my life; my past, my intentions, my choices, my thoughts, my desires, and my reality. Honesty is not just refraining from lies and deceit in relationships with other people; it is about refraining from these enemies in all relationships including the relationship with ourselves.

Recovery was impossible until the hold denial had on my mind was broken. Denial is a good paint job over poor construction. I looked good from a distance. My inner despair was covered with an excellent coat of denial. Denial, while protecting me as a child, had begun to destroy me as an adult. The destruction was like the slow death of a tree. First a few leaves die; then a limb; then a portion of the trunk; then the whole trunk and then the roots.

Denial impedes growth. It destroys the spirit by allowing continued poor behavior and choices to guide your life. Denial allows only the symptoms to be alleviated and not the cause to be treated. My denial blocked my ability to see my past as it really was rather than the fantasy I had constructed. The fantasy served me well for many years, allowing me to survive in a sick environment.

Shame was used as weapon in my childhood. My mother and father both used shame to control or attempt to control behavior of my brothers and me. I never understood how shame affected my relationships until I began recovery. Persistent feelings of inadequacy lingered in my thoughts regarding anything I did. I resented feeling inadequate and would drive myself to seek competency in many areas; many which would later prove to be fruitless in my quest for a peaceful existence. Feelings of inadequacy (I would learn) are a direct result of shame based control. The irony about my parents using shame against me is that their behavior was shameful and while it kept a thin veneer of calm in our house it created a tempest of resentment in me. I've learned in recovery that I've indeed committed shameful acts or deeds and used shame as a weapon just like my parents. However, thanks to recovery, I don't need to drag these around with me and continually seek to justify them. I can recognize the deeds and seek to make amends for them. Also, I don't have to be a victim of anybody else's attempts into shaming me into compliance. Now when I have a feeling of shame or inadequacy I can shine it through my recovery prism to determine whether I've acted inappropriately; taken on someone else's shame or guilt or someone is trying to manipulate me into choosing or doing something that I've set a boundary around not doing. This pause of reflection gives me the time and serenity needed to formulate a response which stays consistent with the principal of "say what you mean; mean what you say but don't say it mean"; rather than perpetrating a resentful inappropriate reaction to the powerful feelings of shame. I work on not changing my feelings but rather changing my responses. This has created a much healthier environment in my home and relationship.

Husband's Perspective on Shame and Guilt

For me, as a corporate man who lived out this whole scenario, it took many meetings and sponsors but by the grace of God I was healed by those tools and the Al-Anon's who taught me how to use them. Shame is so universal among men who live with addicts that I feel we each need to (first) accept it as part of our human condition and second, recognize that as with so many other traits with codependency it is exaggerated.

I felt so good after I had finished my fifth step, and the priest said "...let's face it, you just aren't that good at being that bad!" A detailed description of my fifth step is in a later chapter but for here I have to say that the feeling of freedom I had that night after completing my fifth step out there under the stars; sucking in the cool night air as I leaned up against the car...that was a peace that I will *never* forget. The following quotation is "From Courage to Change, copyright 1992 by Al-Anon Family Group Headquarters, Inc. Reprinted by permission of Al-Anon Family Group Headquarters, Inc."

> *"If I feel ashamed, I need a reality check because my thinking is probably distorted. Even though it may take great courage, if I share about it with an Al-Anon friend I will interrupt the self-destructive thoughts and make room for a more loving and nurturing point of view. With a little help, I may discover that even my most embarrassing moments can bless my life by teaching me to turn in a more positive direction."*

Father's Perspective on Shame and Guilt

Feelings of shame and guilt are often confused with one another and thought to be the same so when writing about one or the other it is important to point out how they differ. Guilt which is held without resolution can become shame but the two differ in several respects.

Shame tells us that we are wrong, bad or worthless while guilt speaks more to our behavior being bad or wrong. Shame destroys self esteem as well as hope and can lead to behaviors which are destructive such as addiction; trying to control others and pushing others away who are trying to reach out to us with love. We become unable to accept love form others and even from God because we feel unworthy of it.

Guilt on the other hand can be healthy because it can motivate us to make amends or restitution for harm that has been done. Once this correction is made and if the motivation for doing so is derived from the knowledge that our behavior was at fault; we can let go of the guilt. It is also important to distinguish between earned and un-earned guilt. Earned guilt is the result of something we have done or not done that is inconsistent with our values. Unearned guilt occurs when we take on responsibility for the bad decisions and choices that others have made.

I have experienced both shame and guilt as a result of living with the disease of addiction. Shame developed at a very young age when I started thinking that I did not quite measure up and that I was inadequate. This thinking and the feelings resulting from it came from being constantly teased by my dysfunctional extended family about having a girlfriend at age six or so. This was in the late 40's and a boy's worst nightmare at that time was to be identified in any way shape or form with girls prior to age 15 or so. They were to be avoided at all cost. There is nothing I can do about what occurred and my reaction to it except to acknowledge what happened and to move on.

My experience with guilt is from having raised a beautiful daughter who suffered from the disease of addiction. I had to accept earned guilt by realizing that I could have spent more time with my daughter during her teen years; that it was wrong for me to rage at her when she came home after using cocaine; that it was wrong for me to control her and that it was wrong for me to withhold love from her because of her actions. These things could have made a difference in her life and I must acknowledge that my behavior toward her did damage. I made amends to my daughter for my behavior and the guilt feelings are slowly subsiding. I also carried a lot of unearned guilt by taking responsibility for all the horrible consequences she suffered from the disease of addiction. I know there was nothing I could have done directly to prevent her suffering and that all I can do is to recognize this as unearned guilt and to let it go. So for me, holding on to shame was destructive while working through guilt is a path to growth.

Heard at a meeting: "Alcoholism is a disease fueled by shame. Shame causes the alcoholic to drink and then the drink brings about shame. We, as Al-Anons, learn to accept this shame by association. I would hear about the antics of my brother in high school from last weekend when he was drunk and feel shame for what he did."

Son's Perspective on Self Pity

Heard at a meeting: "There's nothing more un-masculine than self pity!"

When I am having a pity party I feel trapped. My mind just continues to pass through the scenery of some perceived slight over and over again and I cannot (by my own will) escape the circular trap. Often this starts when I first begin measuring myself against somebody else; whether I imagine myself as superior or inferior by the comparison. Sometimes it starts when another person experiencing pain hurts me and it was really not about me!

What I have done is that I have reverted to the old, pre-program

Scott who is totally in charge. I go back to resuming the God role; where I am somehow wise enough to judge all behavior as right or wrong; all motives as noble or wicked and all actions as appropriate or inappropriate.

My program tells me that I am not the center of the universe; that in God's eyes I am just another child He created and no more powerful (or helpless) than any of His other children. My program tells me that this "stinkin' thinkin' hurts me more than anybody else and that I have to grow past the habit of taking solace in self pity. With my codependency disease self-pity is no longer a luxury that I can afford to indulge any more than an alcoholic can afford to indulge her in escape from reality by consuming ethyl alcohol.

What are some of the losses if I dodge doing this personal work? First, I can only think of one thing at a time so when my thoughts are occupied with self pity I am robbing myself of the very tools I could use to escape the trap in the first place. The work I have done in the past with my sponsor sometimes comes through and I remember his words spoken to me so many times. He says "...don't try to change your feelings; change your behavior."

Finally, I go through the humbling experience of stepping down from my God spot and putting the real God there. Finally, I surrender my will; admit my powerlessness over my own negative feelings built up during so many years of codependency and I ask God to remove the feeling of self pity from me. At that critical juncture, I have reached the bottom of the downward left side of the "v" created by spiraling self pity; turned the corner and begun the climb back up the other side to healthy thinking. I climb that hill like any other mountain climber; by searching for strongholds just within my reach and then grasping them for the next painful inch upward. Maybe a stronghold is the insight that you cannot be resentful and grateful at the same time and I do a gratitude list starting with A in the alphabet and going to Z naming everything for which I am grateful. That exercise alone clarifies the next safe level place just above me. Then there are the steps; I can apply every step to a given difficulty and realize that God is perfectly capable of using my shortcomings to grow me beyond where I was a moment ago. Maybe I apply the Serenity Prayer and realize that the "problem" was not mine to solve anyway. Maybe what I thought was a problem was really God speaking to me with pain to get my attention and then showing me that my fears were natural and right.

Husband's Perspective on Self-Pity

My hitting bottom happened when violence broke out between my wife and me. I had been up with her all night while she drank; trying to convince her that she was not wrong and that her boss was just a bad guy after she had lost another job. My wife had now been fired from three of her last four jobs. The first was a job I had gotten her as a lab tech through a good friend who owned a diagnostic laboratory. He was apologetic when he had to tell me that he had fired her. He said "...because she was just overbearing. All of the techs were complaining that they felt like they were working for *her* and she was the least experienced tech."

The second was another job I had gotten for her. This time they refused to put up with her habitually being late or not showing up because she was sick. She actually had to leave her third job so that I could keep mine. I had to relocate our family in order to keep our main source of income due to a major corporate cutback. My wife never let me forget that one. But now, on this horrible day and night following it, she had lost her fourth job at a hospital laboratory because she had screamed at her boss to "f... off" in front of a room full of employees. As my wife drank, I redoubled my efforts to make her feel better. I protested that "...they just lost the best tech they ever had," and "you can find another job; I know you can...I'll just check around." But she was having none of it. It was as though it was my duty as a supportive husband to reassure her but all that she wanted to do was drink into greater and greater oblivion.

Sometime during the wee hours of the morning, she scared me really bad. She cut the tops of both her arms with a naked straight edged razor blade right in front of me. The cuts were not deep but they drew blood and she certainly got my attention. I remember I couldn't decide whether the right thing for a real man to do was to attempt to take the blade away from her or not. I didn't so I thought of myself as a coward.

As the sun peaked through our living room window my wife voiced one more sarcastic put-down. I could no longer contain my frustration. Fourteen years of it just boiled up and became rage. I threw her by the hair down the hallway. I remember marking off with my steps how far I had thrown her as I stepped down the hall; congratulating myself mentally about how strong I was. This all happened after I had dutifully awakened our children; supervised their getting ready for school and prepared their breakfast. They were sitting at the kitchen table watching this tragic episode unfold while they ate their cereal. In fact, I remember turning to them just before I threw her and calmly saying "...excuse me." This is how insane our lives had become.

I then went into our bedroom, shaking all the way down to my knees from the adrenalin. However, like the good soldier that I had learned to be all of my life, I methodically donned a three piece suit, a white shirt and tie and started driving toward the medical center to work.

But something critically important happened during that drive. I was so upset and I was filled with so much shame at having broken every rule of my upbringing (i.e., "you never hit girls," and "your Dad always said that any man who hits his wife is worthless"). Also, my having done this unspeakable thing right in front of our children was the final degradation. I finally admitted to myself that something was terribly wrong with our lives and that I had to go ask somebody somewhere for help.

Heard at a meeting: "There is life after loss."

PART II.
THE COYOTE'S JOURNEY
TO FIND CHANGE

Chapter 5: The Lies and Finding a Voice

Before embarking on the second part of our work, the recovery process, we need to dispel five gigantic lies that lead to isolation. The lies lead men to isolate themselves from their colleagues, friends, family and other people. The isolation creates a pattern for the codependent male that involves keeping secrets. The lies become patterns of thinking that can literally change his perception of the outside world. This change in thinking becomes toxic or better known as "stinking thinking" and leaves the man speechless.

Husband's Perspective on the Lies and Finding Voice

Lie #1: Big boys don't cry.

Men, we are aware that these words will only reach a select few. We are writing to anybody who has reached their true "bottom" and given up on the whole life process. If you are like us then you were brought to this point by the impact of the two diseases of addiction and codependency. If you have just started reaching out for help through one of the 12-step programs then continue reading. If you are just miserably despondent right now due to these diseases then you might want to seriously consider asking for help.

When we 12-steppers begin to attend meetings we bring our bodies to some point in time and space where other people have gathered who are struggling with problems similar to our own. There is a great deal of hope for us as we walk through that meeting room door for the first time because when our body goes there our mind goes with it. In my case when I stayed for a period of time with an open mind I was forced to accept the fact that there were people there whose problems were at least as great as mine and that they were handling them with dignity.

I learned eventually that it was impossible to hold two totally opposite beliefs in my mind at the same time. For example, I could not continue indulging in childish self pity while being grateful that my problems were not as great as those of another. In open discussions during meetings I heard others sharing squarely where they were emotionally, relationally, mentally, maybe even spiritually at that moment. Sometimes I heard somebody who was demonstrating the self pity right in front of me. Instead of passing judgment I saw suddenly how those words could just as easily have come right out of my mouth! That "A-HAAAA!" moment reduced me to the proper perspective. I had a moment of humility where I made a conscious decision to change my thinking. That was the moment when real change happened. In time after practice, my new "attitude of gratitude" became such a deeply engrained part of my thinking that I became what I was thinking...grateful!

As I began to see recovery, I was able to see that only I could change my behavior and that my actions were mine and not contingent upon anyone else. My old self assumed that I could think myself into right behavior but my new more recovered self came to understand that I have to act myself into right thinking. When the thinking and the behavior matched life became so much easier. I became a better example. My life became a more powerful and meaningful model to everybody around me. The new respect I enjoyed from myself and others came not from my striving to impress but from the fundamental shift in which I *had become!*"

As a man in a 12-step program for people who are being adversely effected by somebody else's drinking, I have listened to men speak during meetings about how hard they are working to overcome such feelings as fear, guilt, and (heaven forbid) ANGER! You think that they will ever really eliminate those feelings? Is that going to happen? Is that even desirable? Here are some questions to ponder; if feelings are sins then why did God make them a part of us? If we had no feelings then what kind of beings would we be? Suppose feelings and emotions are perfectly normal, acceptable experiences for men. Suppose feeling them; expressing them and accepting them for what they are is all OK. Suppose these feelings only cause moral problems when we make the wrong decisions about how to *express* them or how we allow them to dictate our behavior choices!

Life might be a lot easier for us, as well as for those who have to live with us, if we just gave ourselves permission to be healthy emotional men who acknowledge to ourselves and to others that we have feelings. We might even get so comfortable that we are able to admit them out loud to another trusted person (possibly another man) and then let them go until another one happens along. If I feel honest anger toward another person and I have the nerve to tell him or her so and if I am ready to deal with whatever reaction that person has to my honest anger; we might even engage in some conflict. Wow. Wait a minute...is that a sin too?

And here are the two huge payoffs if I do this: first, I form more honest relationships with everybody around me and second, I don't have to stay stuck playing my only feeling over and over again in my imagination. Let me make this so simple that any man can understand it. Guys, ask yourself this question as you finish reading this; how many decades of internal peace have you sacrificed to being mad about something that your Dad did or said when you were only ten years old?

Lie #2: Real men fall on their swords rather than admit defeat.

A wise counselor once told my wife and I, "...it's hard to hug a porcupine!" Addicts and alcoholics are like porcupines. Their decades of consuming known depressants render them irritable and negative. Their addiction has been used to avoid facing and solving life's problems. Therefore, the addict has hampered his or her own maturation process. Maturity can only happen when a person faces a difficult painful situation and then grows enough to solve it. The only true way to achieve this type of maturity is through seeking the advice and even help from those whom you see has a mentor. A codependent does not want to seek help because he or she feels the power of controlling the situation and does not see the error in his or her actions. This is very much like the thought process of an addict. To a codependent, the fallacy is the addict 'should' have control and the codependent cannot see past his own problem. However, loving those who are hard to love is what we are admonished to do. That is a major goal of many religions, including Christianity.

Our 12-step life is riddled with seeming contradictions. On the one hand we are taught not to accept unacceptable behavior lest we fall into the trap of enabling by not standing up for ourselves against those who would abuse us. At the same time we are told to develop acceptance; to release resentments and "to fake it 'til we make it." If you can tease out this distinction...the distinction between the soul of the person exhibiting the unacceptable behavior and the behavior *itself* then it **IS** possible to do all of this. In a sentence; learn the love the person but hate their disease.

Some personify evil as the Devil. Some just think in terms of negative influences in the universe or the yin and the yang. In the Southern states they just say, "...what goes around comes around." But I have learned that negativity is always promulgated by the diseases of addiction, alcoholism, and codependency. That negativity will take away life, dignity, finances, physical health, emotional health, marriages, relationships and spiritual growth. Like a virus, these diseases eventually destroy everybody and everything.

Sooner or later inside every person, choices have to be made that are basic in nature. These are decisions such as "am I going to be a leaner or a holder-upper" of others who lean? Am I going to put forth the personal effort to grow toward self-actualization? Am I going to take what appears as the expedient path or least resistant path and resort to blame; escape through addictions; lethargy and personal stagnation? In the program we learn that these do not have to be lofty questions. Sometimes it is even easier to take the high road than the low one. I have seen people put forth extra effort to lie (sometimes out of habit) when telling the truth was actually easier! I wonder out loud about how often is misery optional. Maybe we have more choices than we realize. Maybe we sometimes choose pain just because it is familiar. Maybe there are better ways to live. Maybe the people who tried to grow us up into adults tried to make us in their own image and maybe that image wasn't too healthy! Then again, you might just want to stay stagnant. No problem; just keep up the conversation with the guy on the bus such as: "Hey man, how 'bout those Patriots?"

Lie #3: *Real men are able to control their feelings.*

There is no point in making this deep or complicated. Let's use a slogan here and just "keep it simple." Let's start with an easily understood emotion. Let's start with laughter. Gentlemen, just ask yourself this question; how long has it been since you totally lost it to laughter? Do you sometimes go an entire day without laughing...a week? Laughter feels good. Laughter comes from a spirit that is light and free. Why don't we laugh more? Is it because laughter requires some loss of control? Is it because you cannot laugh without being in the present? Is it because you just don't see anything to laugh about right now? Addiction suppresses laughter because it renders us heavy and dark inside. There is not space in a mind that is full of worry, fear, doubt, anger and every imaginable projection about what might happen next for lightness of spirit.

Complexity is heavy; simplicity is light. Our slogan, "keep it simple", is profound. Before recovery when having a conversation with someone I perceived as more intelligent than me, I walked away confused. The confusion often led to poor self-talk. Through the program, I have learned that confusion is an elevated state of consciousness. Confusion teaches me. If the confusion is truly a lack of understanding then it can lead to growth. It means that I am still teachable. It means that I am still a work in progress and that I have a personal challenge to rise to some deeper level of understanding of a subject.

I have also learned that complexity sometimes comes because the other individual *wants it that way.* Confusion can also be an internal barometer to identify manipulation or guile in another. I like being around people who are direct. People who are direct never leave you wondering about where you stand with them. People who are indirect are what I call "high maintenance" friends. They require a great deal of energy and focus from me. They have gotten so adept at manipulating others into giving that to them that they do it even while you are aware that they are doing it! People who are deliberately complicated may have underlying messages such as "I am smarter than you are," or "I want you to feel sorry for my situation."

Here is the point; it is OK to laugh like CRAZY whenever you want to do so and no matter what anybody else might think!

Lie #4: Self sufficiency is manly.

Heard at a meeting: "I was taught 'if you didn't fix it you just didn't try hard enough!"

Gentlemen, how often do you ask another man for help...*of any kind?* Before most men can ask for help, it needs to be restricted to a narrow range of male activities. A good example might be working on a construction job. Men working in construction think nothing of asking each other for help because it is just necessary in order to get the job done. If a man wants to move a 4X4 that is about 20 feet long, he thinks nothing of saying something to the guy next to him, "...hey Mac, would you mind splittin' this 4X4 with me? We gotta get it over to the corner there."

However, the same man who was able to ask for help in that situation would not even think of revealing to that other guy that last night he was up with the police until 2:00 A.M. while his 19 year-old daughter was being busted for prostitution to support her addiction.

Here is another dilemma. Asking for personal help, such as the example above, would require a deep friendship between these two men. There would have to be a great deal of mutual trust. My question here is this: Are real friendships between men even *possible* in America today? They were in other cultures; in other times. Take a look at this quote from the Bible and let's explore this issue of deep friendships between modern-day men by comparing them to what the Bible describes.

"After David had finished talking with Saul, he met Jonathan, the king's son. There was an immediate bond of love between them and they became the best of friends. And Jonathan made a special vow to be David's friend and he sealed the pact by giving him his robe, tunic, sword, bow, and belt." **1 Samuel 18:1, 3-4**

First, in the example above taken from the Old Testament, the distinction was made that Jonathan was the king's *son*. That implies that Jonathan was much younger and therefore probably one of David's contemporaries. They immediately had that in common. Our studies of our own Monday Night Men's Al-Anon Group (which has a roster of over 60 men who have attended meetings regularly over the past 12 months) indicate that there is some validity to this commonality among men within similar age groups. The youngest of our group are always in their early 30's and usually have fathers who are their "qualifiers." The oldest, in their 70's, usually have sons or daughters who are their qualifiers. In the middle, the men from 35-55, usually have a wife who is their qualifier. But the disease of addiction transcends the boundaries created by the classic "generation gap." Regardless of age, we watch in awe as the 70 year-old retired coach with the addicted son relates to the 32-year old sociology teacher with the addicted father!

Next, notice what Jonathan willingly gave to David to seal their friendship. First, he gave his robe...his outermost covering. Then he even gave his tunic! Jonathan physically and metaphorically made himself naked in front of David. He said in effect, "I trust you enough to expose myself without modesty to you."

The answer we have learned through years of attending men's 12 step meetings is YES! It is not only possible for men to form deep trusting friendships; it is terribly important that we do so. That trust can be seen by witnessing a CEO trying to describe the sadness, embarrassment, and shame he felt while visiting his only son at the county jail on a Saturday night. It was dead quiet in that Community Center meeting room with the shades closed to the outside world. Those very shades our group years ago bought and donated them to the center to protect our anonymity. The man finally surrendered to his feelings and wept. The acceptance, caring, and just pure agape love that poured forth from the men who spoke after this scion of industry showed how devastating his son's alcoholism had been to him was palpable.

To continue with the theme of friendship in the bible, Jonathan handed over his sword, bow and belt. That meant to me that Jonathan gave up his offense. He handed over all of his protection. He stripped himself of both his means of offense and defense. For a Jewish man of Old Testament times to surrender these items, was the ultimate trust. When our CEO friend wept he removed his front. His pride, bluster, his manliness; all of that which was so important to anyone but especially to a successful corporate man; was surrendered...publicly.

There is another quote I want to use now, this one from Proverbs, 27:17.

"As iron sharpens iron, a friend sharpens a friend."

Reduced by this disease to your core you are now teachable when it comes to recovering from living with or loving someone who suffers from addiction. Teachable means letting go of the feelings after genuinely feeling them and finding a way to move forward to use the skills heard in meetings. Our dear CEO can now attend our meeting for as long as he wishes, trusting and exposing himself every week while witnessing other men doing the same thing. Some day he can develop enough trust to approach a man to whom he can relate and ask him to be his sponsor. The man he approaches may be an auto mechanic, a janitor or an airline pilot. It makes no difference to either one of them. They are men who have learned to trust other men and now the mechanic will serve as the iron that sharpens the CEO.

Lie #5: The capacity to "take it," to endure pain, is what real men are made of.

When James Bond is tortured inhumanely by the bad guy he makes jokes. The *last* thing James Bond thinks, let alone voices, is the words "We admitted we were powerless…"

Men today represent 16% of Al-Anons and yet within the current generation of alcohol and drug users the ladies are matching their male counterparts in addiction rates. Why this huge discrepancy?

When I came into a 12 step program years ago I was one of only about four men in all of a large metropolitan area who attended meetings regularly. Why? Well, first, admitting I was powerless over **anything** was not even thinkable for me; given who I was and how I was raised. A real man does not just accept a bad situation...he DOES SOMETHING ABOUT IT! Second, when I actually did attend a meeting after a sponsor hounded me, I found what looked to me at that time like a secretive little meeting room full of women...most of them much older than I was at the time. Besides, all of the "real men" were across the hall in AA laughing boisterously. Hey, I didn't want to be a 12 step programmer anyway. It was after that first experience, with the help from my sponsor, that I was able to start my life on the path to recovery. This journey to freedom was a direct result of his actions to never give up on me.

Points to Finding Change

There are plenty of causes in this world related to diseases of addiction and codependency which cause by far the greatest amount of human loss and suffering. The reason why is because each person is only as free as the sum of his or her choices. Addiction steals personal freedom. If a codependent alters thoughts, actions and words or stuffs emotions in an effort to defuse a confrontational addict then that person is also a victim of the other's addiction. The slavery to the mind-altering agent has crippled the codependent as well. So how do you change the world? You change yourself with the help of God or a Higher Power through other people in 12-step programs!

God meant for all to *have* free will but how capable are we of exercising it? For the addicted person, his or her disease will eventually take away free will. There will be the inability of the addict to stop choosing the hourly destruction of self...the precious self in the forms of consciousness, awareness and sentience; even thought itself. What could be more precious? Consider such intangibles as memories, knowledge gained, love and their very presence.

But what about us, the codependents, when we allow the others' addictions to render us helpless? We allow a great and awful waste of ourselves. We sacrifice great hunks of our self esteem; options in life; even our very own future. Every gain that we make on behalf of ourselves, our family members and all of mankind is compromised the moment we sell ourselves short due to our codependence. So please ponder the following points and then go on your own very real journey of recovery:

Heard at a meeting "You are only as free as your options. When you say "yes but" to your sponsor you are blocking some options that he is trying to give to you in favor of the options that you know, which are limited!"

Whether you realize it at the moment or not the most important relationship you will ever form is your relationship with your Higher Power or God. Your understanding of a Higher Power or God will deepen with each successive growth step you make by practicing the tenants of a 12 step program.

The next most important relationship is your relationship with yourself. This relationship affects all the other relationships you have; right down to your every day experiences. It becomes a part of an encounter with another driver for a few seconds. You look into his or her eyes at an intersection and you both decide who will go first. That was, though brief and temporary, a relationship. But with the tentacles of addiction reaching out to all members of the family much more important relationships are being damaged. Relationships with spouses, children, parents, siblings and everybody even remotely associated with the family are harmed by addiction.

Your own special flavor of spirituality will grow through such habits as attending meetings, being sponsored and reading 12 step literature. For us, we have found such works as One Day at a Time and The Courage to Change in Al-Anon provide an opportunity for thoughtful grist on a daily basis. Eventually, when you add a daily prayer or meditation with your practice of the eleventh step, your spiritual growth will proliferate into every corner of your life.

All 12 step program work with other people present is twelfth-step work; be it with a sponsor or attending a meeting. That means you will be contributing to the growth of other people as well as yourself. It is at that point when your mundane and "just going through the motions" existence will become so rich that you can hardly stand it.

Not everything in this earthly existence works but the principles suggested here have worked for millions of people in 12 step programs since Bill W. started AA in the late 1930's. As a very wise lady once said during a meeting "...the program is not a fire extinguisher and it is not a Band-Aid. It is a way of life that works in the long term." On a personal happiness level, as each of the 12 Promises come true you will just become a happier more effective individual. This is only an invitation to you. If you want to understand more then you can attend any local 12 step meeting.

Woman's Perspective on the
Grieving the Old Coyote

Being in the field of mental health, I fully understood the textbook version of grief when dealing with the death of a significant person in life. I had explained the process to parents of students and even had a graph depicting the stages of grief in the front of my caseload book to show students after losing a pet or family member. I had even experienced the death of a loved one or friend numerous times myself yet grieving the loss of codependency was like walking in the arctic with only a pair of shorts and t-shirt to protect me. Grief can be a cold place because something so warm and special has expired and there you are left standing in the cold. Grief of losing someone inside my own skin was a totally foreign concept that no textbook or years of graduate school could begin to define to a knowledge hungry person such as myself. It meant moving from trying to think my way through the process to feeling my way through the process. The process is living my life free from the shrouded cover of codependency. The steps are text book in terms but the "feelings" factor shifts because you are not grieving the loss of another human being. **You are grieving the loss of yourself.**

For me, when I fully admitted to myself that I was grieving the loss of codependency it literally had physical symptoms that I was not prepared to experience. The overwhelming, deep pitted, soul shredding feeling would come in waves when I least expected it such as driving in the car; sitting in my office; watching a movie or reading a book. The wave of physical grief would jolt me awake at night from a sound sleep leaving me screaming out loud with tears that were so heavy it felt like sandpaper clawing down my face. Tears would not stop because the deep gut sobbing sound took over my body as I begged God for things to change. At the time I thought I wanted things to be as they were before facing codependency. With codependency my life meant having the dream of a life with all the people, things and situations the way I wanted them. This was the codependent thinking invading me as a way to rationalize the situation. If everything would just stay the same I would be able to control everything. Yet, the physical feelings of grief forced my feelings to take over *my mind*. My mind was a terrible barrier that kept me from experiencing grief in the past for fear of feeling anything for anyone about anything especially if it meant dealing with an addict. For the first time in my life I felt true feelings. Those were feelings of deep sadness; feelings of grief' feelings that have no words to describe. The feelings that consumed my body to the point to where I was momentarily motionless, except for the sandpaper teardrops as they poured out of my eyes, became the beginning of my grieving process. I rationalized away feeling in my active codependency as a way to protect myself from the realities of addiction and my role within the insanity of living with addiction.

Grief is a process and for each it is an individual experience. The process for me entailed physically feeling pain in a nameless fashion in order to move my mind and soul to the next level in personal recovery. For me, that led to dealing with issues surrounding abandonment by my alcoholic father when I was only ten years old. Those issues I purposefully chose to push away because any attempt to identify them would bring back the pain and allow him to abandon me over and over. Identifying and accepting the fact that my alcoholic father and alcoholic ex-husband did the best they could with who they were while in my life at that time, was the biggest spiritual and soul awakening experience. The physical grief opened the vault to issues I thought were of no significance, yet they were indeed the fuel behind the fire in my anger toward addiction. Once I faced myself in the mirror and said, "You are who you are; no matter where you go. So find a way to be happy where you are today" was I able to really heal. That was my final step in the textbook grieving process of acceptance. It was the accepting moment. I will no longer determine my happiness based on the actions of another. No longer will I accept situations that do not allow me to be the independent person I was born to be in order to satisfy another's needs. My needs must come first for me and not in a selfish manner but in a self-caring manner. If I don't take self-care seriously I will relapse just like the drug addict or alcoholic. I too, will not only go right back to the same level of codependency in a relapse but have to consume more codependency to feel that I have control over my life and everyone else who is in my life. Therefore, I take my recovery from codependency as seriously as an addict who has truly come to recovery for him or herself not for the sake of others or to appease a family member. Recovery is truly a shift to self-care.

The Recovery Process: The Coyote Finds Himself

Lastly, before we begin the second part of our book, The Recovery Process, we feel that we should make a disclaimer associated with reading our book. By now, if this book is beginning to touch you, you may be experiencing some nagging discomfort. You may have read enough about the disease process in part one that you can see that you or somebody you love is suffering from either addiction or codependency. Also, if you are like many, you may be projecting that if you enter into some kind of recovery effort this will be a threat to your relationship with the addict who you love. To be blunt, you are right. This program fixes *people*; not necessarily relationships. If you reach out for help you will receive it. That will cause you to begin to change and to grow. When half of any two-person relationship grows the relationship grows but it seldom grows evenly. With a 12 step program; with time and with a Higher Power or God; healing takes place. If the other person in the addict/codependent relationship does not change and grow as well then the two will grow apart. To put it another way, if the addict surrenders and the codependent does not, then both of their recoveries will be difficult. The opposite is also true. If the codependent utterly surrenders to his or her disease and humbly reaches out for help from others then, as we stated above, he or she will receive that help and begin the healing process. This will make the addicted person uncomfortable. Ultimately, once full responsibility for the behaviors associated with addiction is visited upon by the addict without the comfortable cushion of the codependent; the addict will face some difficult choices. Recovery is painful. Growth and birth of any kind is always painful. If the addict either cannot or will not come to a place where he or she accepts the price that has to be paid to gain recovery then recovery will be difficult for everybody in the family.

So, before you embark on your own recovery process, we hope that you will read the remainder of our book. Here you will gain many insights into what recovery involves and how many others have been helped. Is your recovery possible? Most definitely yes; it is very possible. Will it be easy? It will absolutely be a challenge. Will it change the relationship you have with an addict you love? It has for every person we have ever watched who goes through the recovery process so it will change your relationships as well. Will it save that relationship? That change is not up to you. That change is in the hands of your Higher Power or God.

Heard at a meeting: "She can't stop herself; what makes you think you can stop her?"

Chapter 6: The Mute Coyote Speaks

A smart husband is one who thinks twice before saying nothing. That is a metaphorical way of saying "Men don't talk much". Whether you are dealing with an addicted female or not some estimates are made that women say seven words for every one word spoken by a man. There are many references that explain this phenomenon but we like the way Dr. Meg Meeker put it in her seminal work, <u>Strong Fathers, Strong Daughters;</u> "One of the major differences between men and women is how they use words. Women like to talk; men don't. That's just the way it is."

But why is it that way? One reason lies in the fact a woman's brain is anatomically and physiologically better designed for verbal communication than that of a man. Following is an excerpt from a study published by Marianne J. Legato, MD, founder of the Partnership for Gender-Specific Medicine at Columbia University.

She states that *"Men may bemoan women's uncanny ability to remember every word and nuance of an argument weeks later but there's a scientific basis for the gender gap. She continues by stating, "Men and women are different in every system of the body and nowhere is this truer than in the brain." Because of a higher rate of blood flow to certain parts of the brain (including those that control language) as well as higher concentrations of estrogen, women's memories have been shown to be superior to men's in a couple of key areas:* **The spoken word."**

In Dr. Legato's book <u>Why Men Never Remember and Women Never Forget</u> she draws the conclusion that if we were to really think about it, this superior start comes from stories read and through the course of arguments. As a result these things become more firmly fixed in women's memories; are better "packaged" and can be re-called more easily later; again thanks to enhanced blood flow to the brain.

The next is defined under Dr. Legato's terminology of: *"Unpleasant, frightening or stressful experiences."Estrogen activates a larger field of neurons in women's brains during an upsetting experience", explains Dr. Legato. "They experience the stress in greater and more precise detail. Simply remembering an unpleasant incident can bring back the same terrible sadness and agitation to women that they experienced at the time," adds Dr. Legato. She ends with, "On the plus side: Women may be better eyewitnesses at crime and accident scenes."*

As you have read throughout this book, the frustration men experience when engaging in verbal exchanges with women, especially with women who are under the influence of mind-altering substances, becomes a greater challenge. The following is one plausible theory that we can come up with that explains this disparity between the sexes when it comes to the talk-no talk rules.

When archaeologists and anthropologists try to explain how this happened, they point to the agricultural revolution that happened when humans first settled down and started harvesting crops and do-mesticating animals. This happened a scant 12,000 years ago. In the time spans considered by anthropologists studying the history of man as a species, 12,000 years is like the bat of an eye. The greatest period of time *by far* shared by Homo-sapiens was when we supported our-selves as hunters and gatherers.

The women were seen as the gatherers who stayed around the camp with the children. The camps chosen specifically for safety meant everything to everybody. Hollywood has glamorized the hunter in our minds by stereotyping the American Indian, but there is strong evidence to support the notion that the American Indian cultures were dominated by the women. Based on studies of hunting and gathering cultures in existence even today, the line of decent, childbirth, major decisions, even the reliable part of the group's sustenance came through the woman. Recent studies of various American Indian tribes, such as the Navajo, point out that any brave who denigrated a woman, even verbally, was likely to be chastised by the group, while a Navajo woman could give a Navajo man a thrashing in public and place his belongings in front of the hut and that was the last word.

The primitive campsite is where women chatted about any and everything on their minds. The camp was the true site of communication. We can only conjecture that the camp was probably where language was developed in the beginning. It was the perfectly logical place where decisions were made by the members in the tribe. The camp was also a safe place where people could make the noise of expressing emotion through sound with ease. At the camp individuals could scream at each other in anger or laugh out loud hysterically; they could even make the unmistakable shriek made by most primates when startled.

At the camp, especially around a fire at night, the women developed what some refer to as "noodle thinking." This noodle thinking was recently described in a study done at The University of Pennsylvania. Noodle thinking is the notion that thoughts run along one noodle in a knotted mass of noodles until another path looks more interesting, and then the subject abruptly changes. With this system, the conversation can veer off in some totally different direction at any given moment, and other women intrinsically understand this change in direction. It is to our understanding that Jewish women refer to this as the ability to "kibitz," and it is a way that women communicate very effectively. Every woman knows that they are mentally multi-tasking.

They are speaking to each other on multiple levels simultaneously. The conversation might go like this;

"I like your new do. Are you still going to Helen?"

Translation in the male's thinking:

"Let's kibitz, I'm in a friendly mood towards you and I want to pick up at this level where we both have the same hair styles, and we can go off on any number of fun noodles."

Here is how this may have happened by using the following analogy: It is pretty difficult to gather berries, roots, and nuts in the dark, and the natural sex to assume the role of "lookout" or guard is the man. Therefore the scene every night may have included women in varying group sizes engaged in this thinking. Men, in order to function see themselves as the one who does half of the hunting and gathering.

First, hunting is dangerous. In the wild, there is not always that great a distinction between the hunter and the hunted. On a physical level, matched one-on-one, adult male humans are outmatched by many other predators by not only physical characteristics but by sensory perception capabilities such as sight, sound and smell. Because of these realities, men have to be able to focus their attention as acutely as possible for short periods of time. This also requires a totally different style of thinking from that of the women. Men like to focus entirely on one topic and stay there for extended periods while they explore every aspect of that topic imaginable. This may be because during the brief but critically important moments when a decision has to be made in a hunting situation the hunters who have thought through many contingencies have a much better chance of making the right decision at exactly the right moment. There isn't *time* to think the situation through and even momentary loss of concentration can result in loss of the game at best or loss of life and limb at worst!

Communication has to happen between hunters. It can happen sometimes at an almost telepathic level. Simple hand and eye movements, facial expressions, body positions count as forms of communication. Any hunter will tell you that there is a special non-verbal communication that happens between men hunting together. There is also a great deal of cooperation and camaraderie. Everybody knows where everybody else is on a moment to moment basis; their relative ranking among the members of the group; how each man is armed; even his emotional status that day. Also, men prefer hunting alone or in two's (at the most) because they recognize that nothing goes unnoticed in the wild by those who make their living there and the larger the group; the more obvious their presence.

There are countless parallels that have been made by physical, cultural and social anthropologists to the roles of the sexes as defined by the hunting and gathering lifestyle. Men prefer smaller groups and women prefer larger groups. Men detest shopping or any activity that appears to be non-focused and women generally speaking like the browsing that is associated with shopping. Women are much more interested in relationship building both inside and outside the camp and men are more interested in building their own status from within the group of other males with whom they work or hunt.

Given these preferences, it is easy to see why humiliation of a husband by an alcoholic wife in the company of his work associates would be something the man might hate worse than the threat of death. And yet, in corporate America there is still a strong premium placed by top management on a man having the loving, supportive wife. Including wives in corporate functions is still a common business practice. Corporate functions almost always include the consumption of alcohol. That combination to a man with an alcoholic wife is his worst nightmare. There is no way of knowing how many men have been passed over for promotion by having to drag the extra baggage of an addicted wife who brought him shame at the wrong moment during a corporate social function.

Some men resort to their own kind of non-verbal offense/defense.

In the words of John Gray in his work <u>Men Are From Mars; Women Are FromVenus</u> "going into your cave," is seen as the same process. The 'cave' behavior designed to control one's self, if done in a healthy relationship, and provide a brief moment of relief in order to recharge and continue a healthy relationship or face a difficult situation with clarity. If done within the walls of a household hiding an addict, it becomes this dark place that hides everything. The reason this term becomes asked when living with an addict is because the environment within that cave truly is *not safe.*

The Codependent man stays to himself inside this cave because he has learned that his alcoholic loved-one is not trustworthy with his darkest secrets. In a healthy relationship, the time spent in the cave is one that rebuilds the person's ability to communicate effectively with the partner. If the partner is an alcoholic wife, this level of communication becomes a disaster because of the affects of her disease. The cave becomes a hiding place or escape from the pain instead of a place to recharge. The addict consistently lies to him; acts abusively and demeans him creating a sense of being forced into the cave. We have seen the shutting down or 'burrowing in a cave technique' by every man sponsored for a very sound reason. It worked. Closing yourself off does protect you from the addict. That other person loses all power if you do not give them any. Perfected, this device can make life doable in the late stages of alcoholism. If you don't disclose; if you are not honest and open; if you are physically present but not legitimately *available;* then you can minimize your pain. It works for men whether they are the addict or the codependent. This is one key reason why an honest fourth step inventory followed by sharing in the form of a fifth step is so freeing.

Where the cave becomes a healthy way to move through relationships comes when daily unconditional love experienced day after day, year after year, through a 12 step program. This creates a security that is deep and permanent. People are fallible but each has a spirit and many people are genuinely what they appear to be. The early years the coyote spent learning the rules of isolation are eventually trumped by years of mutual respect from sponsors and other men whom they may later sponsor as well as from the fellowship as a whole experienced in a 12 step program. Life becomes a series of the sweetest developments and new habituation replaces old. The sweetness is never ignored from that point forward. It becomes something that is appreciated with each day.

Son's Perspective on Facing the Mute Coyote

I am an adult child of an alcoholic mother. My mother's alcoholism and the effect it had on my life were not discovered by me until I was in my 30's. My wife had started attending Al-Anon meetings and while she was attending these meetings she purchased the book From Survival to Recovery: Growing Up in an Alcoholic Home. I secretly read the book thinking that she had joined a cult. I found nothing cultish in the book but, rather, my story and my family's story being told by many different people. An eerie feeling pressed down on me as I was thinking "how could this be?" I didn't remember any drinking in my family. However, I could relate to the feelings of fear, shame, resentment, inadequacy, anger, isolation and irrelevance that were expressed in the different chapters. I decided that I would attend a meeting to further investigate. There was the possibility that alcoholism was in my family.

My first meeting was on a sunny day in January of 2003. I arrived in the parking lot and headed towards the entrance to the meeting with the following thoughts assaulting me:

"Scott, what are you doing here? You don't belong here! These peoples are wimps! Even if your mother was an alcoholic, how did that affect you? You're smart enough to figure this out by yourself."

The closer I got to the entrance, the more desperate and threatening the voice in my head became:

"What will other people think of you if you are caught here? You will lose your friends if you go in that door! Your mother will be mad if you air her secrets in public, you aren't allowed to do that! What kind of son would expose his family secrets to strangers? You are ungrateful! It could have been worse! I can't believe you're going to embarrass yourself and the family! The past is the past! You need to get over this and move on! You always were an exaggerator and too sensitive! Happiness does not exist, something will always bring you disappointment, and you can count on that!

However, once the meeting commenced with the reading of the Al-Anon welcome the cacophony in my head started to subside. As the members of the group shared their experience, strength and hope I began to feel like I actually belonged. I was a member of many groups; however I never felt like I belonged. Feelings of insecurity and a fear of familiarity kept me from developing any intimate friendships during my life. Yet, here in this dimly lit room, I found acceptance that had eluded me my whole life. I left the meeting feeling better about myself and believing that there was hope for my predicament.

Exploring the Recovery of the Mute Coyote through Questions

Before we leave this section and begin to explore the recovery process for the codependent man, we want to include a 20-question exercise for the reader designed to help you decide whether or not you, the reader, have some of the characteristics of that man and therefore need a twelve step program such as Al-Anon or Nar-Anon. This questionnaire is courtesy of the Al-Anon World Service Office pamphlet "Al-Anon Faces Alcoholism 2008."

1. *Do you worry about how much someone else drinks?*
2. *Do you have money problems because of someone else's drinking?*
3. *Do you tell lies to cover up for someone else's drinking?*
4. *Do you feel that if the drinker cared about you, he or she would stop drinking to please you?*
5. *Do you blame the drinker's behavior on his or her companions?*
6. *Are plans frequently upset or canceled or meals delayed because of the drinker?*
7. *Do you make threats, such as, "If you don't stop drinking, I'll leave you?"*
8. *Do you secretly try to smell the drinker's breath?*
9. *Are you afraid to upset someone for fear it will set off a drinking bout?*
10. *Have you been hurt or embarrassed by a drinker's behavior?*
11. *Are holidays and gatherings spoiled because of drinking?*
12. *Have you considered calling the police for help in fear of abuse?*
13. *Do you search for hidden alcohol?*
14. *Do you ever ride in a car with a driver who has been drinking?*
15. *Have you refused social invitations out of fear of anxiety?*
16. *Do you feel like a failure because you can't control the drinking?*
17. *Do you think that if the drinker stopped drinking, your other problems would be solved?*
18. *Do you ever threaten to hurt yourself to scare the drinker?*
19. *Do you feel angry, confused or depressed most of the time?*
20. *Do you feel there is no one who understands your problems?*

If you answered yes to any of these questions, you are definitely eligible for Al-Anon! We will include information for many sources of help throughout this work, but for this very moment, pick up the phone and call Al-Anon to learn where there is a weekly meeting in your community. The number is 1-888-4Al-Anon. You may also visit their excellent web site at www.al-anonalateen.org.

Father's Perspective on Reaching Out for Help and Denial

I am a father who watched his beautiful daughter suffer from this disease for over 20 years and then received the dreaded phone call on Christmas Eve in 2005 that she had died from drug overdose. My purpose for writing in this chapter is to share what my daughter, my family and I experienced as a result of this disease with the hope that it will help others who are faced with an addicted child. From over 7 years of attending Al Anon meetings twice a week, I have learned some things about how this disease manifests itself. I want to share this general knowledge first and then later discuss how my own story relates to this general description of the disease process. Left untreated, those impacted by addiction experience spiritual, emotional and physical destruction. While the actions and behaviors differ, both the addict and those who are close to the addict follow a parallel progressive downward path. This process usually occurs in four stages.

The first stage of denial is the 'happy' stage during which the addict experiences escape from problems; greater socializing ability and feels in control. This stage often begins when the addict takes the first drink or experiences the first high from drugs and feels that the answer to all problems has finally been found. During this stage the codependent often drinks with or uses with the addict because they are lively and fun to be around. Sons and daughters sometimes drink with dad or mom because they have loosened up and can finally talk to them. These "happy" times are firmly implanted and searched for in the succeeding stages.

In the second stage of denial, some consequences begin to occur and the focus of the addict becomes more directed to the substance. At the same time the focus of the codependent becomes more directed to the addict. Some isolation begins to set in as the addict's relationships are limited to other addicts and the codependent begins to drop healthy relationships because of embarrassment and lack of time and energy. The addict searches for the "happy" times experienced in stage one by drinking and using more but finds that it does not work and both the addict and codependent become even more isolated. The resulting lack of healthy relationships thus begins the process of spiritual decline.

The third stage involves denial on the part of the addict as well as the codependent. This denial is often described as the elephant in the living room. The elephant takes up all the space; makes a mess of the place and continues to grow. Meanwhile, those involved in the addiction process know that the elephant is there but do not openly acknowledge it or discuss it with each other. There is a heroic effort made to hide and cover up the fact that there is an elephant in the room because the addict does not want to admit that alcohol or drugs are the problem and because the codependent feels shame. Emotional decline thus begins with both the addict and the codependent exhibiting similar symptoms. The addict often becomes abusive and neglects responsibilities. They can also become mellow and thus vulnerable to criticism. In either case, the feelings of guilt and of being a victim are medicated with even more drinking or drug use. On top of this, there is still the search to get back to the "happy" times in stage one and the belief that social drinking is still possible. The codependent reacts in different ways depending on personality. Some react by trying to control; raging and criticizing. Others try to be nicer; do even more to fix things; cover up more and help more. Either way the codependent becomes angry, resentful, feels guilt, and emotionally drained. The most harmful of these reactions is resentment. The codependent spends tremendous emotional energy insanely hoping for a better past. The emotional destruction is well underway during this stage for both the addict and codependent.

Serious losses begin to occur in **stage four** including loss of physical health. The health losses experienced by the addict are well known and documented including cirrhosis of the liver, stomach problems, black outs, accidents etc. Less obvious are the physical ailments suffered by the codependent including neck and back problems, stomach problems, coronary artery disease and many others. Most of these are related to stress and the resulting suppression of the auto immune system. Other losses for the addict at this stage include jobs, divorce and financial ruin. The addict continues to drink and use drugs in increasing quantities and frequencies because they continue to be perceived as the solution to the problems. At this point serious accidents, ambulance trips, hospitalizations and imprisonment begin to occur. The codependent has become completely focused on the addict and the problems which are occurring. They are seen as heroes by friends, relatives and neighbors and begin to become severely addicted to some of the behavioral addictions (such as control) mentioned earlier. The downward spiral is nearly complete at this stage and the only remaining options are death from continued use, suicide, imprisonment or recovery. Recovery is only possible for the addict or codependent when they are completely defeated and totally give up the fight. This is called hitting bottom. The addict begins to believe that the alcohol or drug is the problem and not the solution while the codependent begins to believe that **their reaction** to the addict's behavior and **not** the addict is the problem.

The point at which the addict and codependent hit their bottom can occur at any time within the four stages but usually occurs during stage four. Each story or experience, like mine, is therefore a little different from this general description in terms of time and the end result.

Woman's Perspective on being a
Female Mute Coyote

Even within the world of coyotes there has to be a female. There has to be two who contribute! Contributions to addiction are what we as loved ones do without even knowing we are depositing into the abstract account of addiction in life. Yet many deposits or contributions to the development of the muted howls of a lone coyote know no gender boundaries. We ourselves contribute to the noiseless cries by enabling the addict; doing insane things ourselves to control the addict; attempting to help an addict who is not ready for recovery and then living with the rejection and constant relapses while perceiving them as a personal attack on us.

Though females may be perceived as more social beings and talk more to other females; the female living in the grips of addiction in a loved one becomes consumed with muted howls. The muted howls become the noise within our own heads that dictates our function within the pack or leads us to venture out on our own with no clear direction but that of the need to control everything.

Our world begins to shut down for fear of ridicule by friends, co-workers or family members. The reason why is because we, as the loved ones of the addict, are self-appointed holders of the universe. That universe is held together with the gravity of attempts by us to control the addict. Lest anyone see the chaos within our homes or lives, we might lose our outer mask of denial that may be many layers deep due to years of living with an addict. The gravity holding the universe together will shatter if the family secret is exposed and no one will admit that addiction exists in a family member. The female staggers from muted howls within her head to dead silence. It is a silence that deafens the mind; devours the spirit and leads the female to stumble aimlessly through life in a blackness filled with the sound of a murdered dream. Therefore, asking for help means anonymity is a key factor because if the female is exposed she will no longer be able to lift the weight of her world without wondering about the motives of others. In recovery the mute coyote (no matter the gender) can begin the process of pealing back the layers of masks in a safe environment. Here is an environment that will allow for one to see that there is a place where everyone knows the path and has walked the path many times in many directions. The outcome of walking the path is to find that under the layers of masks is an ember of ourselves that can be ignited once we begin to take care of us first. Then everyone else in our lives will benefit from the warmth of the new found flame. This is the true gift of self-less unconditional love; an unconditional gift that we give ourselves that must come from within our codependent selves before we can move through the darkness and regain sound in our lives again. Only this time, the sound heard in recovery will bring about hope, happiness, laughter, and a filter. The filter is what we learn in a 12 step program. To filter what you know you can accept with the addict and other people in your life and know what you have the courage to change with the guidance of God or a higher power. That courage presents itself in a way to change you and no one else.

Heard at a meeting: "Pretty soon you're only frosting and there ain't no cake!

Chapter 7: Coyote Ventures Out with Courage: Attending Your First Meeting

Heard at a meeting: "You're just no longer willing to put that disease on your back and carry it all day long"

With the face of addiction becoming prevalent in society, one may begin to wonder: How many people are attending these 12-step meetings and who *needs* to attend them?

Various studies have been conducted that estimate that about 10% of the U.S. population is addicted to varying degrees to a number of chemical substances including alcohol, opiates, hallucinogens, marijuana and prescription drugs. However, as we have shown so far, what few people realize is that for each addicted person there are on average four other people including family members, friends and co-workers who think they have to "enable" the addicted person. That means that 50% of the U.S. population is being negatively impacted by addiction!

We will identify first three groups of men already involved in recovery: men currently attending Al-Anon meetings, men currently attending Adult Children of Alcoholics meetings and men attending both AA and Al-Anon meetings (so-called "double winners"). There are some 2 million people in AA; the greater part of them men and, according to the public outreach director from the Al-Anon World Service Office, these men are increasingly discovering Al-Anon. Here are recent figures for men attending meetings to recover from their enabling:

Male Al-Anon's in the U.S	20,355
Male Al-Anon's, Canada	2,396
Male Al-Anon's, International	14,734
Total	37,485

Male Al-Ateens in the U.S	3,200
Male Al-Ateens, Canada	266
Male Al-Ateens, International	2,149
Total	5615

Total men in Al-Anon and Al-Ateen in 2003 43,100

Figures for Al-Anon's and Al-Ateens above were taken from a publication of results of a survey conducted by Al-Anon World Service Office in 2003 and published in their survey pamphlet. It is interesting that a more recent survey published in 2006 indicated that men had gone from 12% of Al-Anon's in 2003 to 15% in 2006. In 2009 men were 16% of Al-Anons.

There are several other trends that point to an ever-enlarging male Al-Anon population, including such factors as: the U.S currently has the highest percentage of female addicts in our history, and there is increased public acceptance of rehab, treatment, and 12-step programs. High profile figures are entering rehab daily; many of them young starlets. These people are raising public awareness of a problem especially among younger women. Studies corroborate this impression.

"Compared with men, women with drinking problems also are at increased risk for depression; low self-esteem; alcohol-related physical problems; marital discord or divorce; spouses with alcohol problems; a history of sexual abuse, and drinking in response to life crises." *(M McCaul & J Furst, "Alcoholism Treatment in the United States," AHRW, Vol. 18, No. 4, 1994, p. 257).*

What about that sea of men out there who were raised by addicted fathers and/or mothers? If we look at just addiction to alcohol, the total number of adult children of alcoholics in the U.S is at 28 million, so there are 14 million men who could have their personal loads lightened by attending 12 step program meetings. However, using a more realistic estimate, the one taken from the ACOA (Adult Children of Alcoholics)website, their intergroup offices have registered 1,366 meetings worldwide, with an average of 10 people attending per meeting. That says there are 13,660 ACOA's attending *registered meetings,* however, it has been our experience locally that most ACOA meetings are not registered with any intergroup office!

We are hearing anecdotal information from the women with whom we interact daily that indicate there is a substantial interest among Al-Anon women in this topic of codependency among their male counterparts. Certainly, Al-Anon meetings are still about 85% women and any man who manages to attend one of these is given a great deal of attention! Here are the numbers:

Female Al-Anons attending meetings, U.S. 149, 269
Female Al-Anons, Canada 17, 572
Female Al-Anons, International... 108,051
      Total.. 274,892

Females attending Al-Ateen meetings U.S............................. 5,221
Females attending Al-Ateen meetings, Canada........................... 434
Females attending Al-Ateen meetings, International................. 3,507
      Total.. 9,162

Total women in Al-Anon and Al-Ateen 284, 054

As the decades pass, with the trends currently in place, the male Al-Anon will likely become more common. Women are increasingly coming into AA as the numbers of women with the disease increase. Data today point to a future with ever-increasing rates of alcohol and drug usage among women.

"While significantly fewer adult women than men use alcohol, cigarettes or illicit drugs, among 12 to 17 year olds, rates of female and male use are similar." *(DHHS, Substance Abuse and Mental Health Services Administration {SAMHSA} news release, 9/22/97).*

Lastly, the growth of the ACOA movement (Adult Children of Alcoholics) during the last twenty years as well as other 12-step programs for every addiction imaginable are both trends that invite the emergence of a large group of male Al-Anon. But why are men still only about 16% of those attending Al-Anon meetings?

During the early days of recovery, especially, the male Al-Anon experiences intense internal and external opposition to his "Program." At first, most men are afraid and ashamed to admit that they are even attending meetings. Admitting attendance at meetings is admitting that he has failed in all of his purposes. He has failed to maintain the outward appearances of normalcy…to his neighbors, to the other members of his family, and to himself.

For the lady addict, there is a huge threat to her if her husband shows any changes in his behavior. For example, if he begins reaching out for help through professional counseling; confiding in a trusted friend or relative about what is happening in his home or, God forbid, attending 12-step meetings geared toward his own growth and recovery; then the "status quo" that she has worked so hard to establish to continue her addiction without interruption is threatened. Simply put, her enabler, the codependent man, might do something that would render him not immediately present to attend to her needs. If he begins to change she begins sensing a new attitude and, worse yet, maybe a new behavior. This is unacceptable to the alcoholic lady. If he is actually setting a few minor boundaries and her threats don't seem to be having the desired effect; then for her there is a real problem. Later we will describe the intense need she has for her addictive substance but for the present issue just consider this; for years she has schooled him using both punishment and reward to meet the needs of her addiction and he seems to be somehow unlearning everything. In their game of catch with misery; if he actually starts attending meetings of an organization such as Al-Anon or Nar-Anon, he first stops throwing back the ball, although he is still catching it. After a time, he even stops catching it and that is true detachment. This is a concept that evolves over time and with help from a 12-step program but for his addicted wife, any behavioral changes in this direction are totally unacceptable.

Husband's Perspective on Attending Meetings

Heard at a meeting: "I get fed here. This is where the power is."

It was in this little office in the basement of the Catholic hospital where God arranged for my first sponsor, Scotty L., to walk into the room. It was Scotty who just stayed after me to attend a meeting. I owe him so much today. They were all women; they were all older than I and I knew none of them. I was out the back door without a word to anybody that night. I remember nothing; felt overwhelmed and sneaky at furtively going to this meeting while away from home. I worried about betraying my wife and, most of all, I feared the emotional pain I knew that she would cause me if she ever found out that I had told ANYBODY about her drinking. Thank God, the years and the program have been kind. I no longer have to live with active alcohol consumption in my home and(because of the Al-Anon program) I am surrounded by love every day! If the codependent man overcomes all of the stumbling blocks mentioned so far he has one more hurdle to overcome. This one can be the most difficult of all. He has been trained. The codependent man has been trained by his addicted loved-one's disease to accommodate this person's need for the drug in thousands of subtle ways.

To better understand how this happens to the codependent male, one must look at the biology behind animals because, like the codependent man, animals, too, go through a type of training process that becomes ingrained over time. Biologists have distinct classifications of animal behavior on a continuum from instinct to critical reasoning. Just above instinct is a process called "habituation." Habituation is a sort of non-behavior. It means that some stimulus in the animal's environment results in neither reward nor punishment; so it is ignored. As an example, if you take a horse out of the pasture and put it under a police officer in a major city that horse is suddenly exposed to an entirely foreign environment. The first time an irate driver blasts a horn that animal will be startled. However, after a period of habituation, the horse ignores all horn blasts.

With time, God and the program, a codependent man can learn to trust somebody other than himself. This can be accomplished thorough Al-Anon's fourth and fifth steps. Responsibility for the chaos that the codependent man really deserves is teased out from that over which he was truly powerless since he was a little kid. His inventory includes his **positive** qualities as well. The patience, capacity to nourish other people and hard work ethic that he formed as devices to survive are all still present. The anger, fear, caretaking, worry, lying, over-achieving and shame are all well on their way to being discarded...**because they have been identified**!

Eventually there is growth to the point of being able to *forgive*. The years of resentment bottled up in the codependent man have blocked his contact with himself, with others, and, most tragically, with God. This is one key reason why an honest fourth step inventory followed by sharing in the form of a fifth step is so freeing. Then there is the daily unconditional love the Al-Anon experiences first hand, year after year, through the program. This creates a security that is deep and permanent. People are fallible, yes, but each has a spirit and many are genuinely what they appear to be. The early years spent learning the "system" (i.e., the sick rules imposed by addicted adults and all of the habituations), are eventually trumped by years of mutual respect from sponsors and other men sponsored, as well as from the fellowship of Al-Anon as a whole. Life becomes a series of the sweetest developments and the new habituation replaces the old… the sweetness is never ignored and is always appreciated.

Attachment and Detachment with the Addict: Finding the Courage

One reason why these diseases of codependency and addiction are baffling is because of the complex array of forces attaching the two sick people. Early childhood roles, the clawing need for the addictive substance, the various manipulative techniques employed by both sick partners…all of these forces keep these two people "enmeshed." Because these behaviors developed over a long period of time it is not reasonable to expect them to disappear overnight. Detaching from our closest family members is the most difficult detachment of all. We love these people and they love us. These are the people who cared for us when we were helpless; who loved us when we were not so lovable. They gave birth to us or married us and bore our children. We shared Christmases, birthdays, paychecks and colds with them. We changed their diapers. However, even in the face of all of this history, we can only recover from our sick dependencies upon them when we do the hard work of changing ourselves from the inside out. This is why some sort of dramatic intervention is required to even make a crack in the cement bonding these two. That intervention is always brought about in the end by the pain that both people are suffering.

Pain is the catalyst. On a rational level, the reader might be asking questions like: "…why doesn't the addict just stop" or "why doesn't the codependent just get a divorce?" The problem with such questions is that these solutions do not get to the deep root of the issue. It takes pain to effect change in behavior. All of the facts in the world will not change behavior. Pain will. From the point of view of the person addicted to the substance, no stark fact will change behavior.

We know of an alcoholic man who, after his latest brush with an early death from cirrhosis of the liver, was told that continued drinking would result in sudden death. The doctor literally told the man to make sure that his estate was intact before he took another drink. The man drove away from the hospital, bought a bottle of vodka and was found the following cold morning alone and dead in his truck.

From the point of view of the codependent, we in recovery hear a dismaying array of excuses we call the "yes-buts" from every codependent walking through the door of a meeting for the first few times.

"Yes, but who will take care of her?"

"Yes, but, we need his/her income to survive."

"Yes, but, I swore an oath to love this person in sickness and in health and you just said that addiction is a sickness, right?"

"Yes, but, we are Catholic, and there is no way that our church or our beliefs will allow me to leave her."

"Yes, but, we have been together 25 years and we have already been through so much together."

"Yes, but what would a divorce do to our three children?"

The opposite of attachment is detachment. **Detachment**, because of all of these forces causing attachment, is the core means of survival for both of the sick people described in our book.

You may be asking yourself "But how do I know that he/she is a real alcoholic? He/she doesn't act like an alcoholic all of the time...."

Below are a whole new constellation of reasons why detachment is so difficult for the codependent. Recent literature is identifying an entirely new and terribly difficult addict from which to detach...the high functioning addict. The following, from the Episcopal Church, describes this situation as it applies to the alcoholic but the same dynamic is in place for any addict. The following is taken from literature provided by Recovery Ministries of the Episcopal Church, Inc. and was written by Janee S. Parnegg, CAC. http://www.episcopalrecovery.org/

The family usually sees the first symptoms but is frequently unable to evaluate what those symptoms mean and often attributes them to other causes. The functional alcoholic DOES have personal problems that are caused by or related to the use of alcohol, such as:

Sleep problems	Spiritual problems
Flash anger problems	Financial problems
Relationship problems	Sexual problems
Thinking problems	Emotional problems
Mood problems	Self-esteem problems
Health problems	Family problems
Employment problems	Legal problems
Social problems	

All these problems usually have alternative and very plausible explanations. How, then, does anyone identify a developing addiction problem? Certain things begin to happen and, when examined carefully, a pattern slowly emerges. The following list is by no means complete but includes indications of the types of things to look for. Remember, the alcoholic is often a brilliant super achiever, is employed, and frequently is an admired citizen, right there in the midst of his/her problem.

THE FAMILY SOMETIMES NOTICES THAT THEIR FUNCTIONING ALCOHOLIC MAY:

1. Drink the first couple of drinks quite rapidly but that isn't such a big deal, is it?
2. Fix a drink first thing upon arriving home to relax; to calm

down after a hard day. It seems to be an innocent enough ritual.

3. Require a drink before dealing with any family problems, e.g., Johnny's report card, washing machine breaking down, Aunt Matilda coming to visit, etc.

4. Consume "a drink or two" more even after the others have quit.

5. Have a ritually important night cap "in order to sleep."

6. Frequently seem unable to have just one or two drinks but doesn't seem to get really "drunk."

7. Show discomfort in situations where no alcohol is available, e.g., dislikes going to restaurants where no liquor is served, avoids even fun activities where there is no chance to drink.

8. Make an excuse to leave a party early where the alcohol flows is moderate, even though his/her companion is having a good time.

9. "Draw a blank" about conversations or happenings which occurred while drinking, which would normally be remembered (blackouts).

10. Explain his/her drinking even though no one asked.

11. Make a big deal out of not drinking for a few days, weeks, even months.

12. Make promises that aren't kept.

Part of the denial system of the addict involves the rationalization that "everybody does it". For example, with a legal addictive substance such as alcohol, there are so many powerful forces supporting the alcoholic that are just built into the culture. Teenagers use a phrase something like this; "I'm the only one of my friends who does not party." Alcoholic wives usually have another powerful argument with their husband that often works:

"Hey, look who's talking...I've held your head before while you threw up after a night of partying."

Following is what happened to the husband of an addict when he was faced with this common question asked by the new male Al-Anon;

A Husband's Perspective on His Own Addictions

After about eight weeks in the program, working with my sponsor, I was wondering if my own drinking was offering a ready excuse for my wife. I discussed this with my sponsor and he said that this may be true. He remarked

"…Why not just quit drinking with her and see if she responds?"

I really believed that she would not even notice. For example, we both smoked cigarettes. I had started the process of stopping smoking about two weeks earlier, and she didn't even seem to notice; so I really didn't know whether my drinking with her would be that important. So that weekend, while I did the yard work, I just left off the cold beer.

We had a fight that weekend but I wasn't sure that the issue was whether or not I was drinking with her. We fought constantly anyway. But to my amazement when I started to leave early on Monday morning for a week of work, I found a gift waiting for me on the kitchen counter. There, with a little note were six sparkling green bottles of Heineken beer, my favorite. The note said something like "a surprise for you!" I left the beer there and when I returned the following Friday night I walked into a stinging hornet's nest. She had left the beer and the note there for five days; had looked at it every day and had built up a rage that exploded in a well rehearsed verbal blast at me the moment I walked in the front door. We fought all weekend over whether or not I would drink with her. I guess my drinking with her was an issue after all.

Facing the Addicted Woman

In time, with growth, you make every choice, large and small, on a moment to moment basis in line with who you are. If you don't know who you are, you determine who you are based on outside factors...especially the manipulations of other people. This focus on other people can reach ridiculous proportions. Here is an experience from a man with years in the program that illustrates this point. I remember a bizarre conversation I had one evening before an Al-Anon meeting. We were standing around in small groups doing what Texans call "visiting." I opened with what I thought would be a fairly innocuous question to a woman who had only a few months in the program with;

"...How are you doing?"

She just glanced briefly back at me and answered matter-of-factly;

"He's out of town."

I thought about her answer for a moment and then I asked her again;

"... How are you doing?"

This time she raised her voice, showing some irritation, and repeated;

"He's OUT OF TOWN!"

When I asked the third time she flew into a rage. She screamed at me;

"I am perfectly alright, thank you very much…HE IS OUT OF TOWN!"

I left the conversation with her enjoying the last word and also the stares of nearby onlookers. She was about as *not alright* as possible with codependency. The poor lady had placed so much of the responsibility for her unhappiness upon her alcoholic husband that she could not fathom having a problem without him!"

So how *do* we get it together? How do we find real happiness? First, happiness, I have learned, is neither a purpose nor a goal. One cannot make finding happiness an assignment. For me, happiness comes like a butterfly landing on your head in the woods. That actually happened to me once as I walked through a city park in the depths of despair in my calling-on-the-doctor's suit. I will never forget that miracle. It was just me and God and the butterfly in the woods and I got the message. The butterfly is a commonly used symbol for the Al-Anon program. Happiness, like that butterfly, just cannot be forced.

But is it possible to improve our chances of experiencing happiness? We believe and know it can be done. First, you have to make room for it. You make room for it by stopping the behaviors and thinking that block it. For example, habits like worry, frantic rushing (labeled as 'zooming'), with failure to put in the effort to do some basic planning about how we use our time and sick attachments to other sick people…all of these block happiness. Untreated people lead heavy lives. Everything assumes ultra-seriousness. We see this in newcomers to Al-Anon meetings. To use psych jargon, the most common "effect" in a first-time visitor to an Al-Anon meeting is sadness. Our oral history includes the expression "**hurting people hurt**." That may sound obvious but there is depth of meaning there. Medical professional understand this. Physicians and nurses do not expect light-heartedness or positive demeanors from sick people.

To bring this all together, the program cleanses me from the inside outward. As I become lighter I hurt less and as I hurt less; I hurt others less. As the magic of recovery happens, I begin replacing that bad stuff with good stuff. Eventually I just overflow with the good stuff. I have so much that I am able to begin giving it away and that is how I keep it. This is another great paradox about recovery. **The way we keep it is to give it away.**

For his wife, another disturbing trend is starting to emerge from her enabler. To her frustration, he seems to come home from these meetings whistling like he used to do. About this time, she comes to the perfect solution to this conundrum; *he is having an affair!* Yes, it all fits. The addict wife sees he is spending time away from both his family and his work during evenings and when she learns that these meetings are mostly attended by lonely women; there is this gigantic 'aha' moment for her . So the addict wife begins putting together pieces of a puzzle which she believes to be true. If there are no men-only meetings in the area then a desperate Al-Anon man is forced to attend meetings made up mostly of women. Somewhere deep inside she knows that neither she nor her husband have been capable of providing either the emotional or physical intimacy that they had before the disease progressed. He must be getting that elsewhere.

Husband's Perspective on Facing the Addicted Woman

I remember one of those early Friday night meetings that ended in one of the worst battles we ever had over "my program". After the meeting there was a tradition that those who didn't want the meeting to end would drive across the freeway to a Denny's for coffee. I had never attended one of these social meetings but on this particular night I was invited. I remember standing right outside the door of the meeting room in the parking lot talking to a small group of ladies the moment I was invited to join them. I gladly accepted, much preferring to continue interacting with healthy sober people, women or not, to what I knew by 9:15pm would be a wife with four or five hours of cheap wine under her belt.

Unfortunately, the ladies all piled into their cars and left me alone with this newcomer. This lady proceeded to tell me that her alcoholic husband was not only violent but insanely jealous! I remember imagining him sitting in the darkness across the street looking through a high-powered rifle scope sight at the area just between my shoulder blades. I still had those serious doubts about my masculinity that every male Al-Anon has in the early days of recovery and I was wondering to myself what James Bond would do in this situation? I decided that James Bond would calmly invite the newcomer to ride with him to a restaurant. So that is exactly what I did.

The eyes that I felt between my shoulder blades were not those of a jealous husband. They were those of two women. One was my wife; the other our neighbor who had asked for a ride to the hospital. Deb had told our neighbor the whole sad tale. She suspected that her husband was having an affair with another woman and that they had been meeting on Friday nights at this hospital. To make matters worse I remember the newcomer doing some crying. When I finally came home that night I walked in the front door to the words:

"...I SAW YOU! I SAW YOU drive away with that woman, and our neighbor is my witness!

This went on, again, deep into the night. I remember thinking myself really clever at one point when I told her:

"...yes, yes, I am in love with that woman. I'm in love with her and with every other woman in there! I love them all!

This "affair" which almost every addict wife imagines, allows her to shift the shame from her disease to him. This is where one image of us dies and another emerges.

Heard at a meeting: "Let it begin with me? Let it begin with ME CHANGING!"

Chapter Eight: The Steps of Recovery: Steps 1, 2 and 3

Most of us codependent men do not take step one willingly. Most of us are forced into taking this step by the exquisite pain that we cannot relieve by any of the devices we are trying "on our own." Even the most hardened coyote will abandon his isolation and join with at least one other for support when the question is one as basic as survival. These circumstances are usually just that dire. They typically include catastrophes such as death, incarceration, divorce, bankruptcy or institutionalization. Whatever horror involved, basically they are so painful that they break through our denial. We finally feel the pain. Besides the pain, we feel other things that men as a group absolutely despise: we feel confusion, we feel alone, and we feel helplessness.

Heard at a meeting: "If I have the willingness, I can choose to stop suffering."

We reach step one, sometimes called our "bottom," by different means and at different ages as well. Some are lucky enough to be forced to surrender in their late 20's, usually at this age due to a divorce, job loss, or loss of a parent to the disease. Maybe our alcoholic mother commits suicide or our alcoholic father is refused a liver transplant and we have to stand beside Mom and our siblings in that little room for the families outside the ICU while Dad bleeds to death three doors down the hall with medical professionals running all over the place trying to find a way to plug up the last hole that just erupted in his esophagus.

Or maybe we are in our late 30's and our third failed career-start just ended because we have never been able to work well with other people because of our own unresolved anger issues. Maybe it is an incredible costly divorce with a two-year fight in the courts for custody of our children ending in today's typical outcome…the courts awarding custody of our kids to "the mother." Why, because everybody knows that the kids need to go to the mother; even if Mom stays drunk every night and the kids are left alone to fend for themselves with their homework, local gang pressures, their own poor health issues or just when they need a sober fully functioning parent to spend time with them. In the meantime, they have exactly that in the form of a sober, willing father only a few miles away but he only gets to spend time with them every-other weekend.

Following are real examples of bottoms or the end of the rope. When we take this critical step one, we admit the chaos that alcoholism and addiction has visited upon our life and we even say it out loud to some other human being. That is when we may be directed to a 12-step program. Here we learn that this whole process is caused by a disease. We learn that our alcoholic loved-one is not intrinsically bad and neither are we. But both of us are just sick! That is so freeing. There is a name for all of this. There is no longer a need to blame…anybody. We learn that we did not cause this disease and neither did the alcoholic!

Step 1 "We admitted we were powerless over alcohol and our lives have become unmanageable".

Husband's Perspective on Step I

I'm driving along recalling the horror of those last moments with

Deb; the violence I showed my sons with their own father throwing their own mother down the hall by her hair. But my head is searching feverishly for some solution at the same time. As I'm crawling through the streets that crisscross this giant medical center with my own personal briar patch, I'm thinking "…there must be some sort of referral agency…some specialist who deals with this sort of thing. There must be a solution for whatever is wrong with our family in this massive medical complex!" So, I started with the county health department office. The waiting room was like so many others…eyes of waiting future clinic patients briefly glancing up at me as I came through the door from the chairs along the periphery of the waiting room. There was a nicked up old table in the middle of the room with a matronly woman seated behind it, a sign-in sheet facing me on a clip board.

"May I help you?"
"I need some sort of a referral."
"What kind of referral?"

I feel mildly interested eyes on me now…probably thinking "…this guy doesn't even know what he's doing here!"

"I don't know; maybe some kind of a nurse or something."
"Oh, we have a visiting nurse program for homes. Second door down the hall on your right."
"No, I don't think a home nurse would help us."
"Then what is your problem?"

Somewhere, from some remote corner of the universe, God shouted so loudly that even *my* denial collapsed. Very softly, almost in a whisper, I said;

"I think my wife's an alcoholic."
The old lady couldn't hear me. So she asked much louder;
"What was that?"

I overcompensated because of the profound embarrassment. Mortification in a nana-second busted into anger, and I almost shouted;

"I THINK MY WIFE'S AN ALCOHOLIC!"

The silence in the waiting room just hung there. There was no time. It seemed like nobody was even breathing.

"Oh," she said casually, "you need Al-Anon. They're in the basement of the Catholic Hospital downtown."
"Here", as she scribbled on some drug rep's free scratch pad, "go see the Sister in The Women and Children's Building in the basement."

In half an hour I am sitting across the desk from some stocky nun in full black habit trying to tell her about what was happening last night in my living room when she suddenly interrupted me; came around the desk; took me by the right arm like I was a five-year-old little boy and lead me further down this dark hallway. The sign on the institutional green door said "Al-Anon Intergroup." She opened the door; literally pushed me into the little room and as she closed the door behind her she said;

"Here's another one."

I sat there between two women talking and crying. Talking and laughing. Remembering and crying. They kept finishing my sentences. Somehow they seemed to know exactly what I had experienced and what I was feeling. Then another miracle was orchestrated by that "All-Powerful" one somewhere in the corner of the universe. That green door opened and Scotty L. just walked in.

"Why don't you go to lunch with Scotty here, you guys are both salesmen?"

And that's how it started. There were about four million people all around me in 1976 in a large urban southeastern Texas city, half of them men and to my knowledge only four of them openly called themselves Al-Anon's. With literally million-to-one odds against me, God mercifully matched my first Al-Anon sponsor into that little room and gently introduced me to a means of recovery.

Father's Perspective on Step 1

This title seems, on the surface, to be a contradiction of terms. However, after taking the first step in Al-Anon, I found that infinite power is available to me from a higher power that I choose to call God. The first step states that:

"We admitted we were powerless over alcohol and that our lives had become unmanageable".

When I first heard this step, I did not know what the word powerless meant in the context of the disease of addiction. I could clearly see that my life had become unmanageable but no way was I powerless.

After thinking about the powerless part of this step and all my attempts to fix, control, resent and rage at my daughter's use of drugs and alcohol; I soon accepted on an intellectual level that nothing I had done in the past worked. I continued to behave and react in the same way until I finally also accepted that I was powerless over all the consequences my daughter suffered as a result of her addictions. The last stage of this step for me was to accept that I was powerless over my anger, need for control and resentments (i.e., *my* addictions) because numerous and varied attempts to fix these problems in myself also failed.

Slowly, I am giving up my attempts to battle this disease and have found in those areas where this giving up is at a deep emotional level, God (who has infinite power) has taken control. And so, infinite power is in fact available to me as long as I am willing to accept that

I am absolutely powerless over this disease. Then the barrage of questions becomes:

"What can I do to help my addicted loved one? "

The most important thing is to accept that he or she has a disease over which neither they nor you have control. The addiction, whether it is to alcohol, prescription drugs, illegal drugs, food, spending or sex is fulfilling deep-seated needs created in your loved-one's past. These needs may have come from behaviors within this person's nuclear family long before the person was even in your life; as in the case of an alcoholic wife or husband. After you have accepted the disease concept and stopped screaming, over-reacting, and blaming, you are ready to begin separating the person you love from their disease and all the related destructive behavior the disease is causing. You are doubtless angry with the way you have been treated, mistreated and neglected as a result of these sick behaviors. It is no fun to live with an addicted loved one. Their disease is so cunning and baffling that it has manipulated every person in contact with the addict to feed it, including YOU!

When you begin using healthy behaviors (such as detachment) with love, the setting of firm boundaries or taking better care of yourself on a daily basis; the consequences of the addicts bad behavior will begin to be felt by the addict. That usually causes the addicted person to *redouble* their efforts to regain control over **your** behavior so that you will resume enabling. Please. DON'T GIVE IN AT THIS POINT! Continue with your own recovery. It will take time and great deal of help from others who have "been there" to affect this recovery on your part. There has yet to be any individual capable of doing this by his or herself. This is why 12-step support groups have become so popular throughout the world.

So what is to be gained by my recovery?

Making this basic distinction between the individual and their disease; accepting that distinction and then beginning your own recovery process to extricate yourself from the powerful control the addiction has over you will allow you to accomplish so much. Allowing the addict the dignity to make his or her own mistakes, feel the pain for those mistakes, and learn on his or her own from those mistakes is the greatest gift you can bestow. The direst result for the codependent is: **First, you will cease being part of the problem and become part of the solution. Second, you will allow the addicted individual to find a bottom**. That bottom is the most powerful impetus for your loved one to surrender and reach out for help.

In the AA oral tradition there is an expression that says it all. It goes like this;

"What do you do when you find yourself deep in a hole?"

Answer:

"First, stop digging!"

Woman's Perspective on Step 1

Asking a controlling, codependent personality to admit powerlessness and telling him or her they are living an unmanageable life is like asking the addict to give up the drug of choice. Codependency not only possesses psychological attachments but physical effects that mimic the addict's withdrawal symptoms. The codependents symptoms are ones that, in my case, meant failure to be what I thought others wanted me to become in life. No longer did I own my life but it was directed by my own need for control. I was the one who chose to control everyone including myself into an unmanageable life. Power was my drug injected with guilt upon the addict in my life being the accelerant. A needle that was never clean but laced with expectations and demands that left unfilled by the addict was the push into my veins with the after effect of resentment which has a climax effect of anger and darkness. At least living in the grips of codependency I knew what was coming up next. I could predict everything; granting me more of what I considered control over my life and the life of the addict. In reality it was shear insanity.

Once I began to see how others in a 12 step program functioned within their given lives I could begin the process of letting go in increments to my addiction to codependency. Only then was I able to see addiction clearly and that a whole, good, complete person was underneath the shroud of complex feelings that controlled my life. Controlling life is the polar opposite of changing life. No matter where you move your mind, your heart, or your body in life, you are always in the same place. It is in the strength of clarity of the glasses that we choose to put on that shows us how to live within the life given to us without a choice. Therefore, admitting powerlessness means wearing the right clarity of strength in your glasses and having the courage to admit you can no longer manage your life as a single entity. Only by acknowledging that life can be lived under the control of a Higher Power and not the control of yourself, are you able to be present and live a life free of codependency.

Step 2: "We came to believe that a Power greater than we could restore us to sanity."

Son's Perspective on Step 2

I used to pray to God all of the time as a little boy that my Mom would stop drinking; that Dad would be happy and that my step brothers would stop using me as a punching bag. I would ask myself the question "...what kind of God would make a little boy grow up in this place?" The God part of Step 2 was almost impossible for me to accept because by the time I was a grown man I had made myself into my own god. My plan was to become so successful and so rich and important in my job that I could call the shots. This is why I became absolutely driven. I also always believed that I had to know everything. That driven personality did not make me a very well liked person sometimes. In fact, I was eventually driven to step one, not by the obvious addiction of a close family member like so many others in the program but because of the behavior that I had developed in response to all of the dysfunction of those who had raised me. That behavior kept me miserable inside; isolated me and just before I hit my bottom, was threatening to end my marriage.

After taking all of the steps and working with my sponsor, I realized two important misconceptions that I had the first time I read the second step. First, I read the step to say "...came to know that a power greater than myself could restore me to sanity." I have learned that I can believe something without having to know it in my mind like the answer to a math problem.

The second realization that I have made is that before recovery I actually did have a God. In fact, I had many. My gods were money, success, respect, influence, fame and "stuff." I have also learned that, as a man, I was not alone worshiping those things. These things are God-substitutes for many men. By definition an idol is any object of excessive devotion or admiration. Looking back at what I was willing to sacrifice for those things, it is obvious that my devotion to grabbing them made them my false gods. That style of life was truly insane and I am grateful now to the program for bringing me back to sanity.

> Heard at a meeting: " If you go to Sears Hardware looking for a loaf of bread you will leave disappointed. If you continue going to Sears Hardware looking for bread, you can choose to stay mad at Sears Hardware forever, or you can choose to go to a bakery!"

Step 3: "Made a decision to turn our will and our lives over to the care of God as we understood Him."

Father's Perspective on Step 3

This is the only step where we are asked directly to make a decision so it implies that we have the power to do so. How do we get this power? The only way is to admit defeat and to believe that God can restore us to sanity (steps one and two). When I first read this step I thought, OK, I will make this decision right now so I can move on to the next problem. This kind of thinking, I learned later, meant that I immediately tried to take control again. It took me about two years in Al Anon bouncing between steps one, two and three (known as the Al Anon waltz) before I understood that turning my will over to God was not a one-time decision. It was a way of living my life where I must make this decision many times during the day.

Making this decision continually does not imply that I don't have to make other decisions. God has given me an intellect and expects me to use it to make decisions when necessary. I do the homework; pray; make the best decisions I can and then leave the outcome to God. This works a lot better than the old way where I would focus on the outcome with anxiety and fear which robbed me of the clear thinking required before making the decisions.

Another thing I have had to learn about the first three steps is that they are never going to be completed. It is part of my nature to want to take control and I often slip back to the old behavior and thinking. The good news is that when my self-will gets me in trouble, I have the first three steps of Al Anon to get back on track.

Why Can't Guys Trust even God?

Step three in every 12-step program reads: "made a decision to turn our life and our will over to the care of God." The step admonishes men to do what for most men is impossible...to trust a power beyond them. As the title of this chapter suggests, those two words: "**trust God**," are actually an elegant summary of the first three steps of AA or Al-Anon. After the agony of the diseases of addiction and codependency force us addicts and codependents to take step one admitting our powerlessness and after we accept the difficult terms of the second step (coming to believe that a power greater than ourselves could restore us to sanity) then we are ready to "bring it on home" with step three.

It has often been said that the 12-steps of recovery are simple but difficult to do. Step three illustrates this principle in spades. For men, the third step is especially difficult because we are men. We were born male into a culture that in many cases imposed prerequisites upon our manhood that are almost impossible to meet. For example, as grown men we are expected to know how things work. This does not just include mechanical things. We are expected to answer questions about how people and the world operate. We are expected to have answers. Because of this, *not knowing* is difficult for men. When we don't know something we consider that our very masculinity is in question.

Looking deeper, what happens when we men come up with an answer and then are told by an abusive addicted loved one that we are wrong? Being right is terribly important to every man but especially a codependent man who has many issues about self esteem. Such a man is geared to respond to any difference of opinion by taking a stand and defending that stand "to the end." Given this attitude, he is really in an impossible position when facing conflict with an addicted loved one. Here is why. Addicted people are hurting people. They are not therefore by nature flexible especially when it comes to any change in their circumstances. If that change threatens the addict's access to their favorite addictive substance then the intense need for the substance will redouble the opposition to anything negative anybody says about their addiction. For example, what follows the words "why do you have to drink so much?" from a codependent husband to an addicted wife? The answer is simple. Those words are a prelude to out and out warfare! So this is the typical impasse; the insecure man who has a huge personal investment in being right is squared off against the addicted loved one who equates losing her addictive substance with death.

Before recovery, back in the mute coyote days, the solution to any problem we men faced was to think the problem through and then correct the problem exercising our intellect and our sheer will. We knew that we could change our economic status, our level of education, other people's reactions to us, even the shapes of our bodies using these powerful forces. We knew this because we had solved many problems in our pasts using this system. It worked. However, intrinsic to this system was the need to constantly pass judgment. How can you know that your will (i.e. all of that *effort)* works unless you compare the way things were before to the way things are after you have exercised it? Therefore, when we come to step three, a common approach for us codependent men is to revert back to that tried and true combination of intellect and self will to "make it happen."

"Hey, I can do this."

This is why step three is so difficult. The very essence of the step is to turn our wills over to God. The word *I* in the sentence above is the crux of the problem. After we begin recovery, we begin attending these meetings. Here we are helped by others who have taken this step. Here we are confronted with the simple truth that this is not a self-help program. This is a surrender program. This is a program that requires us to do what we can to make the internal preparation but in the third step we have to leave the outcome to a source that is beyond our intellect and will. That source may use methods that we do not enjoy. That source might use methods that are even beyond our own imaginations. We cannot fix this by just getting a bigger hammer. This step cannot be forced.

But how do we know that real recovery is happening through our Higher Power and not, maybe, even through some unconscious level; through those old devices that are so familiar? The following is a three question system that I have developed to answer this question.

"Was it God's will or was it mine?"

First, when God is doing something, I am surprised by both the process involved and the outcome. If God accomplishes something by means that are outside of my imagination then I know that my will was not involved.

Second, I know if the outcome is far better than what I had originally tried to accomplish. So many times in my life I have been amazed in retrospect to see where God had actually done for me far more than what I had anticipated when I asked for help.

Third, if nobody is harmed in the process. This is the criteria that will likely be contested by others. Yes, I know that sometimes God accomplishes His purposes and people appear to be harmed in the process. All I am saying here is that in my experience, when the effects of the event are ultimately known, everyone is blessed when it was God's will. What may appear to be harm to a person may actually be the best possible outcome for that person. For example, nobody enjoys being chastised but if you see chastisement more as a *pruning* process then you might see where chastisement, in the end, is a blessing.

Here is an example that applies to your codependency. If you learn about and grow past your enabling behavior then your addicted loved-one is likely to experience some pain brought about by their behavior. That pain might be the only way that God can get their attention. That pain may eventually lead to the addict's reaching a bottom. That pain may be the best possible mechanism to drive the addict towards recovery.

Heard at a meeting: "I've learned that if I'm in a funk about something then I have to do something different."

Chapter Nine: Cleaning House. Steps 4, 5, 6, 7, 8, 9

Heard at a meeting: "Have you noticed that you are going through growth cycles alternating with comfort cycles?"

After taking the first three steps begin steps 4-9, the "cleaning house" steps; it is not a matter of choice if you are at all committed to recovery. It is just not possible to stretch to a higher level of consciousness if you are burdened beneath a half of a lifetime of shortcomings.

The fourth step inventory presents a "once-in-a-lifetime" opportunity to pause in your daily life of coping with the tyranny of the urgent to pause and peer carefully back at every situation that caused you to evolve into the person you have become. Few people *ever* have the chance to take responsibility for what they have done or not done with their life in the middle of it! Responsibility is the exact opposite of blame. Responsibility looks forward to eventual betterment of the self; blame looks backward, searching for anyone who can be blamed for every negative outcome.

Taking the fourth and fifth steps, writing out a searching and fearless moral inventory of yourself and then admitting your shortcomings to yourself, to God and to another human being is *not easy!* It takes a huge reservoir of trust and faith and it feels like the first time you jumped off of the twenty-five foot platform at the pool. It is scary;

exciting and, at the same time, freeing. As people in a 12 step recovery program who have enjoyed the "cover" of an alcoholic whose behavior was so obviously bad for years; we find it especially difficult to take that plunge and take full responsibility for our own stuff. Low performers will blame a poor life outcome on *anything* other than themselves, and alcoholics make the handiest scapegoats.

The supreme irony is a direct relationship between the level of responsibility you are able to accept for your own life outcome and how much real control you have of your life in the future. In every area of your life where you take full responsibility, whether it is responsibility for your finances, your relationships, physical and mental health, your moment to moment happiness or your spiritual connection, that area will become more free. Peace of mind comes only when that past is acknowledged, accepted and eventually corrected in areas where you fall far short of what Your Creator had in mind when you were made. You were not *made* with negative behaviors and emotions. You had to learn them and anything that can be learned can be unlearned. We love children for their innocence, for their spontaneity and for their whole-hearted joy in just being alive. We were all that way once and we can be that way again. Meaning "…you are to become as little children."

By taking an honest and open fourth step inventory you tease out your own responses to the situations life gave you; not focusing on the situations but your reactions to them. You are forced to locate those tough areas from your past where you have always hung tenaciously to innocence…where there is absolutely no way you are going to accept any credit for what happened.   You have to find the areas where your attitude has always been something like this;

> "…but who wouldn't react that way. Look at what she did to me! Look at the way she ruined my life. If I hadn't had to marry her, I could have…", or "…I was the victim here…It wasn't my fault," or "…but my Dad abused me; we were poor; we were the wrong race or religion, or political party."

All judging of another person will eventually lead to isolation and loneliness. A judged person has a strange power over us. If we have judged them they *own* us! We have chosen to be offended. We have used what the psychologists call "identification." We have attached ourselves to that person with a smelly attachment cord and their garbage has been pumped into us. That is why so many Al-Anon meetings are led on the topic of "detachment." Detachment is the deliberate severing of that dirty cord. With personal strength, we don't need to take in their negativity. If they have been rude or hurt us in any way, then that is their stimulus. We still have ultimate control over our *response*. Everything is dependent upon your response to a situation not to the situation itself!

For an elegant description of how powerful this kind of control is read Dr. Viktor E. Frankl's classic Man's Search for Meaning in which he describes how people in Nazi concentration camps were sometimes able to find a measure of personal freedom even under the most appalling of circumstances. Frankl's logo therapy, which is the heart of his theory, states that human beings are searching not so much for pleasure in life as for meaning.

To summarize, it is in those areas where you cannot or will not accept responsibility for your part in what lead to the poor outcome that are precisely the areas blocking you from finding the meaning in life for you. Identifying them first and then actively working to dig them out like weeds and eliminate them; is an exercise allowing personal growth to restart in a stagnant life.

Step 4: "Made a searching and fearless moral inventory of ourselves."

Fathers Perspective on Step 4

After working the first three steps it became apparent to me that the only thing I could do was to begin working on myself. Step 4 was an action step which I needed desperately because working on me was what I needed to replace working on my addicted loved ones. Working Step 4 also allowed me to separate feelings of guilt which were justified from those that were not justified. Recognizing the **3 C's** (did not **Cause** it, can't **Cure** and can't **Control** it) helped me make the separation. The behavior changes I made after working Step 4 benefited me and improved my relationship with my family and friends.

My initial approach to working Step 4 was analytical in nature. I listed faults and did a root cause analysis for each fault identified. After this attempt, I filled out the Step 4 Blueprint for Progress notebook which was still an analytical approach for me. Both approaches were educational regarding Step 4 but did not identify character defects that were based on my feelings. The next approach was to list all the people I had feelings of resentment and anger toward; write down what caused these feelings and then write down my behaviors that contributed to the problems with these relationships. The behaviors that were identified occurred in each of the relationships with the people I listed. This made me realize there was a fourth C which was my contribution to the disease.

After working Step 4 by identifying feelings, my charter defects became obvious. They were the need to control; preach and lecture; solve problems; judge others and avoid getting emotionally close to my addicted love ones. I spent an obsessive amount of time at my job site because it was a hiding place which allowed me to avoid the interactions with the addicts in my life. I kept my distance from the addicts in my life to avoid getting hurt by their disease related behavior and their emotional/physical injury from the disease.

Heard at a meeting: "Pain is inevitable; suffering is optional."

None of these character defects helped me or the addict. In fact, they were enabling because my addicted loved one's reacted to my behavior by using it to justify using drugs. Others react to their addicted loved ones by doing more for them and helping them get out of the problems that occurred because of their addicted behavior. This is the classic definition of enabling or codependent behavior because it provides a safety net for the addict and helps them justify using more drugs.

The way we react to addiction varies depending on whether we are primarily right or left brained in our thinking. My thinking is left brained because my reaction to the disease of addiction is to solve problems that the disease generates for the addict and for me. Those who are right brained focus on providing more for the addict and doing more for them. In my case, my left brained orientation was greatly amplified when my loved ones became addicted. This amplification also occurs to those who are right brained.

Part of working Step 4 is to list the positive character traits and to recognize that many of the negative character defects can also be positives. Solving problems and helping others are both positive characteristics if they are not used excessively when reacting to an addicted loved one. Balancing the left brain and right brain behaviors makes both of them very positive in our relationships with our addicted loved ones and others. In my case, the character traits of solving problems; getting facts; staying organized and controlling myself (not others) were both positive and negative traits. It is critically important to list our positives in order to be able to change the negatives. A negative character trait cannot be removed unless it is replaced with something positive.

The biggest benefit working Step 4 had for me was that it changed my focus from solving my addicted loved ones problems to solving my own. Ironically, sometimes working on ourselves helps our addicted loved ones get into recovery from their disease. My obsessive left brained approach to solving the addiction problems for my loved ones did not work. Doing this seemed to make the addiction worse and certainly increased my frustration, anger, resentment and feeling of guilt.

Step 5: "Admitted to God, to ourselves, and to another human being the exact nature of our wrongs."

Husband's Perspective on Step 5

I always tell my "sponsees" who are having trouble starting their fifth step that there must be at least one of the entities in this step that you do not trust yet; God, yourself or another human being. Once you figure out which you don't trust and ask God to put that trust back in you then you can take this step.

But why put forth all of this effort? Well, one key reason is that you will become a free person. Here is a quote taken from an Al-Anon at a meeting today. "You will be freed to begin putting more time, energy and thought into becoming the person God had in mind when you were created because you will stop investing these most valuable commodities into keeping the secrets of your past."

Another reason is that life will get easier. Try carrying your household garbage around with you for a few days and that will show you how "not-free" carrying garbage makes you! Taking a thorough fifth step with a trusted person after your shortcomings have been laid out in writing during an honest fourth step inventory is a way to throw out a bunch of garbage from your past. It takes a huge amount of personal growth and humility to even reach the point where you are capable of considering these two "housecleaning" steps but once you do them; it is done. Garbage only has to be discarded once if you really allow God to haul it away in his big green truck!

As a review for you "non-steppers", by the time we reach this step we have already admitted that we were powerless over alcohol; come to believe that a power greater than ourselves could restore us to sanity; made the decision to turn our life and our will over to that power and meticulously written out a thorough inventory of both our faults and our assets. You will be freed to begin putting more time, energy and thought into becoming the person God had in mind when you were created, because you will stop investing these most valuable commodities into keeping the secrets of your past.

Heard at a meeting: "Contentment only comes when my wants are not as important as God's will"

Lastly, just stop and ponder here how this garbage metaphor holds up with extension...how does garbage smell? To give you perspective before and during your fifth step, here are 14 ideas and points to ponder:

1. Say a prayer FIRST, OUTLOUD, AND TOGETHER when working this step with a sponsee. This lets you both know who is really in charge!

2. If I fear this step it is probably because I do not trust one or more of the three areas in the admitting process - to God, to myself to another person.

3. Humility is the key - admitting to God first and surrendering our will to Him.

4. Arrogance, self justification and resentment can conceal other faults.

5. Ask, how do I react to people in my daily life (self focused, distant, uninterested, not joyful and needy for approval) and why do I react this way?

6. What situations have power to hurt me?

7. When admitting to another person, talk about how we feel about our faults and how others have responded to what we have said or done. Try to avoid judging of self when doing this.

8. Should self pity be on my list if it is not?

9. I must love myself unconditionally just as God does.

10. I must learn to trust others more.

11. Ask your sponsor time and again towards the end of the experience "...is there anything that we may have missed?"

12. What basic unmet childhood need was operating when we behaved as we did?

13. Let go of the need for perfection and become HUMAN.

14. If I can let my sponsor know me, can't I also do the same with others?

Here is a story to better illustrate the fifth step in recovery.

I had just attended a meeting and was standing in line at the cafeteria next to Charlene, a woman for whom we all had huge respect. Her husband, her qualifier, had been all over the news as he was a well known executive at one of major Atlanta corporations who had just been indicted for fraud. Charlene was one of those ladies I considered a "black-belt-Al-Anon." She was direct, honest and had a big heart.

"So, have you taken your fifth step yet?

There it was. A direct question the way only Charlene could ask it.

"No, I haven't gotten around to it yet."
"Why not?"
"Well, I've had my fourth step hidden in the garage for over a year now and I just don't want to go dig it out and start that."
"Do you have a sponsor?"
"Yes, but he is so busy and so am I!"

I then regaled her with the incredible work load that I was handling. I was managing two other reps in the south and covering sales for the major teaching hospitals. I was also, in my spare time, setting up and monitoring drug studies for the research department. To which she replied with something like:

"…they have really qualified priests at the Catholic Church who hear them all the time, why don't you give them a call?"
"Well, I'm not Catholic, and …I don't know the number."

That was about as lame an excuse as I had ever used, even to myself. I said it with that tone of irony that John F. Kennedy used so brilliantly with that famous lady reporter who always seemed to ask him the tough questions and it got a big laugh from the other ladies in the line. But even my clever self-effacing humor bounced off of the shell of the indomitable Charlene. The conversation continued:

"No problem," she said. "Here."

She reached into her purse; pulled out a little book and held it up with the page showing the phone number for the Catholic Church right in my face. Then she pulled off a close that any salesman would have applauded with gusto with the following:

"There's a pay phone right over there by the door. Do you have a dime?"

All of a sudden, I had no place to hide. Inside, I knew it was time. I remember just going into that strange zombie walk with God that I have since learned to accept. My legs were walking over there to that phone, and I knew that I had to just keep moving (Just don't stop). Charlene and several other ladies were drilling holes into the back of my jacket as I dialed the number. Suddenly this priest, whom I had never even met, said as casually as if he were asking for the time of day...

"...can you be here tonight at 7:00?"

This meeting went well into the night filled with reading and laughing; reading and crying; talking; and answering the fantastically pointed and probing questions from the experienced priest. He kept filling the silences when I would sort of "run down" with the question;

"What else?"

I poured out everything and more. He even pulled stuff out of me that I was not willing to write down while doing my fourth step inventory. Some of these qualities were terribly shameful, yes, but many were qualities that I had developed in the course of surviving alcoholism that were genuinely admirable.

When it was over it was well past midnight. After the last long pause, he broke the silence by asking if I would hand him the little music dictation book. When I did, he matter-of-factly tossed it into the trash can beside his desk. I came right out of my chair!

"But…"
"Don't worry, the janitor won't read it," is all he said.

I see now the wisdom of what he did. The past is the past. It is over now. Today really was the first day of the rest of my life! I will never forget the feelings I experienced that night standing out next to my car under a big Georgia sky. The Church is, yes, in a residential/commercial part of Atlanta. But it is surrounded by natural forest and during that long quiet time standing by myself among the tall trees I felt more free and more at peace than I had ever felt in my life.

Step 6: "Were entirely ready to have God remove all these defects of character."

Woman's Perspective on Step 6

This step has wording that, for some, may have a negative con-notation. If you take a realistic look specifically at the word **defect** it sounds like a broken or rejected person. By this point in step work you are a broken person who is mending with each step physically and spiritually. Maybe being a reject or broken person is true but another possible way to view this step is to say, "I am entirely ready to have God or my higher power help me re-write all the rules in my life." So the word defect becomes the word "rules" and the connotation becomes more of a lesson than a brutal curse.

In our lives we are aspired to a certain set of rules that either come from our parents, family members, coworkers, bosses, friends or through a series of life experiences. These rules are what govern our character and guide our actions. The rules then become ingrained to the point to where every situation is determined by how it fits the rule we have about ourselves and those we encounter daily. These rules cloud our judgment and create a hostile environment within ourselves while fueling the aura of insanity when we are faced with addiction in a loved one. It is not until we see that we are living and loving an addicted person and how codependent we are upon him or her, do we see our rules and how they have hindered the progress of recovery not only for ourselves but for the loved one. This does not mean we are rejects or horrible people for living by the old prescribed set of rules. We did not fully create the rules on our own. Therefore, when Step 6 comes into play, we are asking God or our higher power to help us rewrite the rules in our lives. We must also not discount the truth that old rules will indeed reappear when a new situation presents itself. It is when the old rule reemerges that we really begin our work in rewriting and living by the new, healthy, non-codependent rules. For me, once I accepted the truth that I was a codependent person, I was able to see my old rules and then rewrite them in a fashion that I knew supported a life without constant regrets, guilt or abstractness. The old rules were the following:

1. I do not exist without someone/partner in my life.
2. I do not feel safe unless I am in a relationship.
3. If someone loves me then I am safe.
4. How I will react is determined by the actions of others.
5. Words spoken by a person are what I believe at all cost.

The identification of the old rules came from looking at my hierarchy of needs in order to feel safe. To go back to the actual words of Step 6, these rules were my character defects that stemmed from abandonment by my alcoholic father and then subsequent life with an addicted ex-husband. For me, codependency meant safety. Therefore love, attention or affection, even if it was laced with alcohol, meant safety. The old rules said that I cannot live with myself without being defined by another. There was the golden of all old rules or character defects for me; safety meant relying on someone else to provide safety for me; not for me to provide safety by myself. It was an expectation or responsibility that I was asking someone to fulfill for me. That is the true essence of codependency; the defining ourselves by external factors or other people.

Next developed the new set of rules to live by and acknowledge as a part of my life after codependency. Much like the addict, we codependent personalities must set up a relapse plan. A part of the plan in codependency recovery is to redefine ourselves based on the acknowledgement that the old rules were unhealthy and that only through the assistance of God or a higher power are we able to be guided to discover the new person within our own skin. The rules changed to the following for me:

1. **I exist.**
2. **I can choose to love. Love does not define my safety.**
3. **The actions of another do not define me.**
4. **The words of another do not define me. Words do not express me but my actions do.**
5. **When all else fails remember number one.**

The tone of the rules changed because my outlook on life changed by working the sixth step. By looking at the old rules and seeing how they influence our reactions, we become proactive in ensuring our own personal recovery. In this discovery, I was able to define how the rules or character defects entered my life and how they gouged upon my soul for a lifetime. Only then, when I was free from the old rules, was I able to accept the person I was, the person I am, and the person I will become in life. This opened the door for me to see that I am, in fact, teachable and not fully present in my life without the guidance of God or a higher power. I was able see that each person I encountered from that point forward was a part of a teachable moment that yielded a path for me to live out my new rules. When the old rules would emerge it was like facing the old rules ogre in drag clothing. No matter how your dress it up, it is still an ogre. No matter how you look at it, the old rule is still there; it just appears in a different way. Recognizing that the ogre will appear in different clothing meant being present in my life and seeing that old rules or character defects will never go away. These old rules will just morph themselves in your life under a different pretense. How we handle the ogre is dependent upon how confident we are that our new set of rules or character traits gives us a path to a new response or possibly no response if necessary. The character defects or rules once identified become a choice. Do I choose to live by those defects or old rules? Or do I choose to face them; learn from them and feel confident within my own skin? That is the power behind Step 6 in a personal recovery program; freedom from the old self and a celebration of the new self.

Step 7: "Humbly asked Him to remove our shortcomings."

Heard at a meeting: "I may not be able to disassociate myself from my thoughts, but I know that I can disassociate myself from my mouth."

Husband's Perspective on Step 7

By the time I took this step I had done an amazing amount of introspection. I remember my old self, and that old self would have read this step as some platitude loaned to me by a coach or a parent, like "...pull yourself up by the bootstraps," or "clean up your act", or, in '60's parlance, "get it together, man!" I knew that I could depend on the God of my understanding to remove the shortcomings. All I had to supply was the asking.

The sixth step left me willing, and my fourth and fifth steps had given me easy references to identify my short-comings so I started there. These were not pretty characteristics that had crept into me. I saw over and again in my fourth step such short-comings as impatience, a harshly judgmental attitude, uncontrolled lust, and a carefully honed ability to lie whenever the truth was not expedient and just plain laziness. It helped when my sponsor told me that I did not have to ask God to remove all of my shortcomings at once and that I could get started now and continue the process for a lifetime.

One thing I have noticed with these shortcomings; they tend to come back. They are like those little gophers in that arcade game that pop up and you have to drive them down with a big wooden hammer. Every time I whack a shortcoming down to a level where I at least cannot see it staring at me, another pops up right next to it!

Humility's Role in Step 7

- Absolute humility would consist of a state of complete freedom from self; freedom from all the claims that my defects of character now lay so heavily upon me.
- Perfect humility would be a full willingness in all times and places to find and to do the will of God.
- Humility means getting down to our right size and stature so that our self-concern and importance become amusing.
- Humility is not a state of weakness but of strength and being teachable.
- In humility we possess self-esteem, accept ourselves as we are, assets and defects alike, and extend the same acceptance to others.
- Humility means balancing God's responsibility with mine so that we become a team.
- Humility is not putting ourselves down or denying our strengths; rather, it is being honest about our weaknesses.

- If you think you have humility you don't really have it.
- We are humble when we become totally willing to accept God's help.
- Humility is an attitude of honesty and simplicity along with a mindset of being teachable.
- Humility amounts to a clear recognition of what and who we really are, followed by a sincere attempt to become what we could be.
- Humility is honesty and depth of vision, a realistic assessment of us and our part in the scheme of things.
- Humility places us in a true relationship with a Higher Power and with other people.

We will end our writings on the seventh step with the words of Bill W., the founder of AA. These are taken from the daily AA reader As Bill Sees It, p.106.

"Perfect" Humility

For myself, I try to seek out the truest definition of humility that I can. This will not be the perfect definition, because I shall always be imperfect. At this writing, I would choose one like this; "Absolute humility would consist of a state of complete freedom from myself, freedom from all the claims that my defects of character now lay so heavily upon me. Perfect humility would be a full willingness in all times and places, to find and to do the will of God."

When I meditate upon such a vision, I need not be dismayed because I shall never attain it, nor need I swell with presumption that one of these days its virtues shall all be mine.

I only need to dwell on the vision itself, letting it grow and ever more fill my heart. This done, I can compare it with my last-taken personal inventory. Then I get a sane and healthy idea of where I stand on the highway to humility. I see that my journey toward God has scarce begun. As I thus get down to my right size and stature, my self-concern and importance become amusing.

Step 8: "Made a list of all persons we had harmed and became willing to make amends to them all"

Father's Perspective on Step 8

Working Step 4, where I focused on all those who I felt anger and resentment toward, helped me generate the amends list. The reason Step 4 helped is that in addition to listing those I felt anger and resentment toward, I also identified what part I played in the problems within these relationships. Since I contributed to the problems, it was logical for me to include these people on my amends list. Step 4 also helped me to specifically determine what harm had been done by looking at my character defects. The amends list included three columns which were the names, relationships and the character defects that were harmful in the relationships.

My list included all family members and also included some friends and job related co-workers. The list was prioritized with addicted loved ones first followed by other immediate family members, extended family members and co-workers. Step 4 helped me realize that I needed to make some amends to my daughter immediately and that waiting until I reached Step 9 was not adequate. Much lower on my prioritized list were people I had feelings of anger and resentment toward but could not identify any character defects that related to my relationship with them. Some of those listed were those who I had no intention of making amends to at this point. I was not willing to do so as Step 8 states but nevertheless, I listed them. I was reminded that this step simply involves making the list and not making amends.

I also included God on the list because some of my character defects affected my relationship with God. In order to accept God's forgiveness, I needed to include myself on the list as well because I needed to recognize that all the guilt I felt was not justified. I needed to forgive myself for the way I reacted to the disease. I did not react the way I did because it was my desire and my nature to do so. I reacted the way I did because part of this disease is contagious. My behavior and the addict's behavior are both impacted by the disease of addiction.

One of the barriers to developing the Step 8 list is that I was not ready to make amends to them all. This barrier was removed by focusing on simply making the list and asking God to provide the will power to make amends and the opportunity to do so without worrying about the timing.

Step 9: "Made direct amends to such people whenever possible, except when to do so would injure them or others"

Father's Perspective Step 9

My list from Step 8 was prioritized based on which people were damaged the most. My daughter was at the top of the list and I made amends to her for some specific character defects long before reaching Step 9. These included my criticism, being judgmental of her, trying to control her and detaching from her as my daughter rather than detaching from her disease.

A specific amend I made long before reaching Step 9 was my reaction to her after she seriously relapsed on cocaine. I criticized her and preached and lectured to her while driving her home from a hospital emergency room. Looking in the rear view mirror, I noticed the tears she was shedding while she apologized. At this point it became clear to me that she had a disease, did not want it and could not control it. I knew that I needed to make amends to her and did so a short time later. All the amends were not made at this point and she died from the disease before I completed making the remaining amends. The Al-Anon program suggested that it helps to make amends to loved ones who die from the disease by writing a letter addressed to them. Writing the letter helped me a lot and I now have a very close spiritual relationship with her.

After making amends to my daughter, I made amends to the rest of my immediate family members. There were several advantages and surprises in doing so. My sons did not react negatively or positively which confirmed to me that the amends were needed. In addition, it helped open the door for sharing with each other about personal problems. The disease of addiction in my family resulted in members who were not addicted to exclude personal sharing within the family. They indicated that sharing their personal issues would increase the burden that I had with the addicted loved ones.

Making amends to God was also done and was much easier because I worked Steps 2 and 3. These Steps did wonders to improve my spiritual life by helping me recognize that one can be religious but may not be spiritual at the same time. Even though I have not yet made specific amends to myself or to all the people on the list, having more of a spiritual life motivates me to do so. Making amends to me is a gradual process and I will need to continue to work the program to do so.

I have not made amends to some of the people on my list because I have not yet identified any faults related to my relationship with them even though they were people I felt anger and resentment toward. I intend to keep them on the list in the event that God sets up a need and an opportunity to make amends to them. Making amends helped me eliminate my guilt feelings and improved my relationship with those I made amends to. One of the significant side effects from the disease of addiction has on families is isolation from others as well as from each other. Making amends helped us become more open to others and to each other.

Heard at a meeting: "I am a recovering fixer."

Chapter Ten: Helping Others, Steps 10-12

When you first read the steps, you don't realize that steps 10 and 11 are as much a part of helping others as is step 12. Steps 10, 11, and 12 are sometimes called the "maintenance steps." Ten keeps us clean today so that the shortcomings identified and worked through in steps 4-9 do not creep back into our thinking and lives. Step 11 is so profound that thousands of mystics have devoted their lives to each word in it but it really boils down to staying spiritually fit.

If you have flown on an airliner and heard the directions from the stewardess, you might have noticed that she always advises the parents to put the oxygen mask on themselves before putting it on their children. That basic wisdom says; "hey, if you die; so will your children!" In the same sense, those of us working Step 12 on a daily basis know intuitively that we must continue our daily practice of Steps 10 and 11 to keep ourselves emotionally, mentally and spiritually healthy or we will die and have nothing to give to others!

Step 10: "Continued to take personal inventory and when we were wrong promptly admitted it."

Husband's Perspective on Step 10

The 10th step is an each day inventory. Below is a written 10th step done in the "feelings log" that my sponsor taught me to use as a tool to maintain my sanity. Maybe by reading this you will have a better feel for the depths of this addiction disease, and some of the costs to those "other four" who have to work so hard to hold up the addict. You become what you teach. For some sound reasons, we Al-Anon's refuse to give advice. **And that means ever!**

One night while attending an open AA meeting, God spoke to me through an AA member with only a few months of sobriety. The AA member, like me, had developed the habit of practicing his 10th step at night just before going to sleep.

He would lay there and go through his day thinking through each incidence where he had been wrong and/or had harmed someone else. He would then acknowledge this to God and to himself, and promise first thing in the morning to make a 10th step amends to the person wronged, which he did.

The AA member, newcomer or not, had gone one step further than I had with this step. Taking his cue from the word "inventory" in the step and remembering that his very healthy sponsor had insisted during his fourth step inventory that he include the *positive* aspects of his character as well as the negative, he made the leap from today's unhealthy habit to tomorrow's healthy one. He acknowledged to God and to himself each incident during the day when he had *successfully* aligned his will with that of God. He said that this daily habit kept his real spiritual purpose in front of his mind on a daily basis. The habit made him feel like he was a "co-creator" with God, with God providing the inspirational thought, and him carrying it out.

Before falling asleep each night, the AA member savored and cherished every small seemingly insignificant miracle where God had just "serendipitously" placed him in situations with other people where he was given the *opportunity* to do God's will and he had actually done it!

I thought of a beautiful lecture I heard once by Brian Tracey, in which he developed the concept that it was impossible to develop integrity by yourself. The 10th step inventory allows us to participate actively with others in our mutual growth. When I buck up and summon the nerve to approach another man and say something like "… hey, I'm glad I bumped into you here at Wal-Mart." "Listen, I have to tell you that I am sorry about the other night when I took that cheap shot at you about your hairline." "I got a laugh from the guys but it was at your expense and I've felt bad about it ever since."   That speaks volumes to the man to whom we are admitting we were wrong. That is like the knight who approaches the other knight in the center of the bridge and holds out his hand in friendship. That is saying, "…hey, I have no concealed weapon and I trust you enough to leave myself open to you if you choose to take a cheap shot in return." That also is the real stuff of intimacy. That allows both of you to admit that you have flaws, and that there exists enough trust between you to allow each to be vulnerable in front of the other. That also challenges each of you to change for the better. If you have disciplined yourself to practice the 10th step, then you tend to think more carefully about your behavior because the embarrassment of making an amends is no fun!

But what have you done to help him? You have taught him by way of example. You have grown before his very eyes, and you have demonstrated that growth. He has been given the opportunity to be magnanimous, to forgive. How often does that happen in each lifetime? To borrow another quote from Brian Tracey, "…the teaching is in the words but the learning is in the silence." The man you have blessed with your amends will likely spend some silent time contemplating what happened in that Wal-Mart aisle!

Heard at a meeting: "I have learned to live life right today instead of trying to correct it tomorrow."

Step 11, "Sought through prayer and meditation to improve our conscious contact with God *as we understand Him*; praying only for the knowledge of His will for us and the power to carry that out."

Notice that this step does not read "Sought through prayer and *medication...*"

Hey, don't laugh. There must be a reason why alcohol was once referred to as "spirits." We need not belabor here the long history of people using various substances to induce specific spiritual experiences. Even your great-great grandmother recognized this. Guess what was the favorite elixir during her time, and is still enjoying brisk sales all over the world? It is Lydia Pinkham Elixir. Lydia Pinkham has many herbals known to improve mood, reduce, stress, etc. but it also contains 10% ethyl alcohol "as a preservative." There are many other preservatives available now for manufacturers to use other than ethyl alcohol but this preservatives makes Lydia Pinkham's Elixir 20 proof or about half again more potent than table wine!

Step 11 is late in the order of the 12 steps for some good reasons. It requires long-term spiritual growth through the other steps to reach the point where you will actively strive to improve your conscious contact with God. Each tiny phrase within the step represents a concept and spiritual endeavor that has been studied and practiced for millennia by sages from every religion. But for here, let's view reliance upon God from a more modern local perspective.

What Is Your Source of Authority?

When Max Weber (often called the father of sociology) first described the three basic sources for all authority the first he described was what he called "tradition." Tradition borrows authority from the vast past of all man's recorded history. Tradition basically perpetuates the laws in all legal systems; dictates "proper behavior" and represents "behavior that is considered *safe*."

More than one text has summarized this source of authority as "Father might; father right." Isn't it interesting that men fit so easily into this four-word summary for authority! Has anybody ever considered how much pressure that places on men? With this system in place in the minds and hearts of so many people of all ages and sexes, it falls upon us men to define authority; to be right and to maintain stability within the society. That is no small load to carry!

The next broad category of classification for sources of authority according to sociologists is rational thought. Max Weber, like most of us born and educated after the "age of reason," placed rational thought above other sources of authority. The founding fathers of The United States of America were all proponents of reason as the ultimate source of authority so they based their authority to form a new nation upon reason instead of tradition. It was reason that gave them the authority to oppose the traditional authority of the British monarchy.

The final source of authority, according to the sociologists, is what Max Weber termed the "charismatic." Because he was himself a rationalist (i.e. all of the "ologies" are based on authority from the rational or scientific), Max Weber had to define anything other than the rational as the irrational. He recognized that there was something beyond the rational that had authority but he had to define it in negative terms because he was so enamored with the rational. Into this third category the sociologists lump such forces as intuition, the emotional, the creative and, ultimately, that which is spiritual.

We are providing this background because we have learned that there is actually a fourth source of authority that often trumps those described by the great thinkers. That is the authority that is assumed by the twin diseases of addiction and codependency. This authority is the addictive substance or behaviors that maintain the addiction. The only "right" supporting this authority is anything that allows the addiction to continue working its devastation. If you attend a local Al-Anon meeting where family members gather to grow and hear our stories, you will come to appreciate that there is no question about the power or the "might" half of the equation when it comes to addiction.

A man brought to maturity within any one of the authority sources generally accepted by sociology experiences deep frustration when confronted with the authority assumed by these diseases. For example, a man who was taught to operate within the authority of tradition… the man who understood that "…father might; father right," is in an impossible position when he comes up against the chaos visited upon him by these diseases. Tradition is one of the most powerful sources of authority *assumed by addiction*. In families where addiction has ruled behavior for generation after generation, any man who, for example, refuses to drink alcohol might have to pay a huge personal price in the company of his own nuclear family members.

Now consider the man whose source of authority was based on rational thought. He, too, will come up against a solid wall of authority when he tries to apply logic to confront the authority of addiction. It makes absolutely no "sense" to continue swallowing a known poison and to experience all of the pain brought about by the dysfunctional behavior caused by the addictive substance. It makes no sense to watch those he loves as they die excruciating early deaths after having been impaired for decades by their addictions. But if he appeals to logic to justify his refusal to join in lock step like the proverbial lemmings marching over the cliff as he, too, experiences the losses imposed by addiction; he will pay huge personal fees in the form of abandonment and ridicule.

All that is left for Authority that has even a ghost of a chance to overcome the authority of addiction is the spiritual. Whether you realize it or not, right at this moment there is a mystic Power within you that is perfectly capable of bringing you into recovery. This Power is there, whether you believe it or not, and you will be neither the first nor the last to discover it. We have witnessed too many come into our meetings filled with despair, sarcasm, doubt and really seemingly impossible life circumstances. With time and the God these people find among us, they are lifted so far beyond their circumstances that within a year they are hardly recognizable. Through the recovery process that has evolved naturally in response to the agony of the addiction disease…thanks to the greatest power of all…you can all find your true self and your rightful place in the universe. This is your birthright. These diseases are so powerful that no person can overcome them alone. We literally need divine intervention.

Step 12: "Having had a spiritual awakening as a result of these steps, we tried to carry this message to others and to practice these principles in all our affairs"

Father's Perspective on Step 12

Relapse for those of us who are codependent is likely and working Step 12 helps us refocus on the other steps, the slogans and our spiritual nature. Sponsoring others has helped me recognize my need to continue working the program and helped my understanding of all the steps. This is especially true for the first three steps. The person being sponsored struggles with the first three steps just as I did when I first started the program. Hearing the struggles that the person sponsored has experienced is a reminder of the thinking that kept me from admitting I was powerless, that only God can help me and that my will and my life must be turned over to Him.

The slogans are tools that I use to prevent relapse and to recognize when I have already done so. Whenever I am tempted to control, preach and lecture and become judgmental, I use the "Let Go and Let God" slogan. Working Step 10 every night, I recognize whenever I have already relapsed into the character defects and make amends the next day. The slogan "One Day at a Time" helps me deal with Step 10 on a daily basis and start each day with a clean slate by making amends. Sharing how the slogans have helped me at meetings is very powerful in helping others because it provides a means to deal with a crises, frustration, guilt and anger.

Starting a new group (Nar-Anon) reinforced my belief that the Al-Anon and Nar-Anon programs are miraculous because of their spiritual nature. The amazing recovery that others make is what keeps me working the program and going to meetings because without exception, those who make progress do so because their lives have become vastly more spiritual.

Working Step 12 enabled me to make a transition from enabling behavior to helping others in ways that are spiritual and positive in nature. It's almost impossible to stop the enabling behavior unless it is substituted by some other means of helping others in our lives. In addition, working Step 12 helps us to provide some pay back for all the benefits we received from the program. This results in a very satisfying and spiritual feeling.

Heard at a meeting: "We have to learn to be normal again... if we ever were."

Chapter Eleven: Tools for Recovery: Living in the Real World

Our lives, like many others, have been a testimony to the truth that pain is something we must endure to see the true gifts of our Higher Power. The first half was guided more by reaction than action and more by habit than by carefully thought-out design. Let's address this issue of habit first since it is probably the most important factor blocking the changing of behavior for the better.

We know now that, more than anything else, we are all guided on a moment to moment basis by habit. Habit cannot be changed by simply willing that change to happen. One important principle we have learned is this; the best way to change a less than ideal habit is to replace it with a new and better one. This is doable because, luckily, the mind can only think one thought at a time.

Attending an Al-Anon meeting at least once per week might rob you of some mindless "entertainment" hours in front of the tube, but until you do it you cannot possibly imagine the journey of growth it will initiate, saying nothing of the hugely expanded network of closely intimate friends. The information below briefly encompasses what you will find in almost any 12 Step Recovery Program.

The slogans

When you enter an AA club or an AA or Al-Anon intergroup office you might see various slogans posted around the walls. They say things like:

Easy Does It	*Live and Let Live*	*Just for Today*
Think	*Let Go and Let God*	*Listen and Learn*
First things first	*How Important Is It?*	*Keep an Open Mind*
One day at a time	*Keep it simple*	*Let It Begin with Me*

A Woman's Perspective on Slogans

Slogans are what one lives by when life gives you no explanation and leaves you in a state of shock filled anger. They become an answer in the barrage of events in life.

Heard at a meeting: "Beware of urgency, because urgency is usually my will."

When life becomes a mystery of hard times associated with an addict or other difficult people for that matter; they become an additive to life. Slogans replace all the other codependent thought processes that attempt to eat away at your life or your day. They become the positive answer to things that have no answer. They can become the avenue to the light at the end of a very dark cave that has consumed every ounce of who you are as a person. It can be a way of God or your Higher Power providing insight into something that is void of sight. They are words to live by; forever.

Husband's Perspective on the Slogans.

When I first saw the slogans I thought they were way too lame. I mean, I am a reasonably bright guy; what could something with so few syllables mean to me? I'm really *complicated.* Then one horrible day, the day when I was scheduled to go through my annual performance review with my manager, I had a major GI bleed-out due to the combination of stress ulcers and oral steroids prescribed by my doctor for my asthma. I lost almost half of my total blood supply that morning; some of which ended up in the floorboard of the rental car that my manager used to drive me to the emergency room at the nearest hospital.

Losing whole pints of blood through vomiting in front of your manager (with both of you wearing your best suits and ties) just is not funny but, in truth, bleeding ulcers is common among family members who live year upon year under the stress of addiction.

What did those simple slogans mean to me that morning?

They meant everything.

Son's Perspective on Slogan's

When I first heard the "Let go and let God" slogan I thought it meant just go into a state of not being present. I now know it means much more than that. For me, letting go of people was at first almost impossible. I was a controller. I always acted; said and did everything with an agenda. I was always scheming about how some person who was important to me (like my Mom) would react. When you are a little kid, you think of your parents as having supreme power over you and you are right. I learned early to use every device I possibly could to manipulate my parents into treating me good. Especially in my Mom's case, it was all so that she would not *leave,* but Mom did that anyway. She would tell us that we kids had ruined her life and then she would just leave. I remember a scene where she was going out the door holding a packed suitcase and I was holding onto her leg crying and begging her not to go. This is why I understand on a deep level how Adult Children of Alcoholics have serious abandonment issues. For me it was not just emotional abandonment through the use of alcohol; it was real abandonment... like walking out and leaving the kids to survive at home until Dad came home from work.

I see "Let Go and Let God" on a deeper level now. I see letting go of my expectations of how others will react to me. I see "letting go" as letting go inside myself of the need to control another. I have to give up all of the stories that keep repeating in my mind of how I was abused as a boy. I have to let go of the need to "figure out" why my parents treated me so badly. I have to let go of that gut-wrenching *fear* and replace it with healthy more realistic thoughts. I have to say to me "...it's not going to be the end of the world if my worst fears come true." I have to let go of my need to always know what is going to happen tomorrow.

Day-to-Day Living in Recovery

We men are planners. We really do look at a pile of stones and see a cathedral. We are therefore very seldom in the "now." One big advantage for men in staying out of the now is that we don't have to feel feelings that way. If we are living with active addiction in somebody for whom we care then the real now is filled with feelings that are negative. We have to feel our anger; then our fear and maybe even our sadness. Here are some thoughts on living in the now.

Living in the now is all that we really have. The program's oral tradition sometimes refers to the past as a cancelled check; the future as a promissory note and the present as ready cash. The horrors of addiction and codependency are real enough. They often make the present miserable. It is therefore more comfortable to dwell on the past or project into the future. However, if we fall into that trap we are giving up our most precious commodity...our presence. That is why living "One Day at a Time" is such a freeing way to be. Staying in the stinkin' thinkin' of the past or worrying about a future that is not likely to even happen makes no sense. It requires hard work and years of disciplined healthy living to unlearn this habit but what is the alternative?

The Do's and Don'ts of Day-to-Day Living.

Somehow the concept that men do not like to ask for or follow directions has crept into "common knowledge" during the last couple of decades. I wonder how that happened. I mean, how can we guys be engineers, physicians, professionals, or chefs if we cannot or will not follow directions?

The Al-Anon program has several sets of directions and we have come to love them because they *work*. When I first came into the program the twelve steps felt more like theory to me than directions. They sounded so lofty. They looked so formidable; like a mountain with its peak so far above the clouds that I couldn't see them. But there was a set of directions that I could and did access from the very first day. These were the Do's and Don'ts. I heard one man say at a meeting "…my life started getting better when I just stopped doing the don'ts!" These simple directions are so important that they are listed in the "Our Stories" part as described by the head of a large family riddled with addiction ("A Special Christmas Letter from Dad"). At this point, you might want to turn to either section and see how powerful and true those "Do's and Don'ts can be for you.

The 12 Promises in Daily Recovery

Taken from <u>Alcoholics Anonymous</u>, Third edition.
(The Big Book).

1. We are going to know a new freedom and a new happiness.
2. We will not regret the past nor wish to shut the door on it.
3. We will comprehend the word serenity.
4. We will know peace.
5. No matter how far down the scale we have gone, we will see how our experience can benefit others.
6. That feeling of uselessness and self-pity will disappear.
7. We will lose interest in selfish things and gain interest in our fellows.

8. Self-seeking will slip away.
9. Our whole attitude and outlook upon life will change.
10. Fear of people and of economic insecurity will leave us.
11. We will intuitively know how to handle situations which used to baffle us.
12. We will suddenly realize that God is doing for us what we could not do for ourselves.

The Three A's: Awareness, Acceptance and Action in Daily Recovery

We will finish our chapter on the tools of the program that illustrates how to use the 3 A's in a dangerous crisis, in the short-term and how a lifetime of using them can finally rescue you and those you know and love from the downward spiral of addiction.

Father's Perspective on Life in Recovery

Prior to making any hasty decisions after learning your child is addicted, it would be beneficial to remember that we are ill equipped to deal with numerous issues that are involved in addiction. You need to get your child help either through a 12 step support group, professional addiction counselor or both. Along with your child's recovery, you need to seek assistance in dealing with the pain, uncertainty, fear and insanity that are normal for parents of addicted children. The first healthy thought you should engage is that you did not cause the addiction; you can't cure the addiction and you can't control the addiction.

Some specific things you can do:

1. Focus on creating a healthy emotional atmosphere in your home. Resist the urge to yell by focusing on saying what you mean; mean what you say but don't say it mean.

2. Focus on improving yourself and not on curing your childs addiction.

3. It is important for both parents to work together by setting boundaries that define what will and will not be allowed in your home along with the consequences of behavior that is not allowed.

4. Be patient and don't resent the method of recovery. Recovery of the addict may or may not materialize and chances are that if recovery does occur it will not be a result of what you did but rather it will be the result of another addict doing 12 step work with your child while carrying the message of experience, strength, and hope.

5. Keep a sense of humor and gratitude. These help when dealing with crisis.

6. Remember that your child has a higher power. Fortunately, you are not it because you are powerless over the disease of addiction. This frees you up to focus on your recovery.

7. Maintain hope that things can get better. This hope will keep you sane and help you with your responsibilities.

8. Do attend a 12 step recovery program for codependents and do get a sponsor. You will find out that you are not alone and that there is help.

So, this is not the way you thought the family history would unfold when your child was born. Resentment, shame and anger are probably consuming your thoughts when you see your child. By following the steps outlined above, however, and making a commitment to the recovery process for yourself, you will find serenity, joy and freedom whether your child's addiction continues or not. Often, the child also gets into recovery after they see the changes in your behavior. Addiction resulting in recovery may be the impetus to get your life restarted and refocused on the things that truly matter such as service to others, compassion, acceptance and honesty.

Proof That Addiction is Indeed a Disease

If you need proof from any person as to the fact that alcoholism is a disease, following is the description of the disease taken directly from The Merck Manual, the "go to" research source for most physicians to find a description of all known disease states. This concept can be applied to any addiction. "The development of characteristic deviant behaviors associated with prolonged Alcoholism; dependence on alcohol; consumption of excessive amounts of alcohol. Alcoholism is a chronic illness of undetermined etiology with an insidious onset, showing recognizable symptoms and signs proportionate to severity."

"The discussion of alcoholism needs two separate foci. Consumption of large amounts of ethyl alcohol is usually accompanied by significant clinical toxicity and tissue damage; the hazards of physical dependence and a dangerous abstinence syndrome. Additionally, the term alcoholism is applied to the social impairment occurring in the lives of addicted individuals and their families." (The Merck Manual, 14th edition).

Chapter Twelve: A New Spirituality.

Heard at a meeting: "I think I used everything else as my God: my kids, my house, my money."

People who are living in dysfunctional addiction/codependency riddled families sacrifice more to their diseases than any of them realize. The sacrifice of financial stability, emotional security, interpersonal trust and personal peace are well documented in mental health circles as well as by the media. These are bad enough but all partners in the addiction dance...the enablers and the addicts, engage in a kind of self-surrender that is even deeper. They sacrifice their very experience of living in the moment.

For example, how many special childhood memories have been destroyed when either or both parents are alcoholics? The child with alcoholic parents very early in his or her life adopts a kind of hypervigilance. Because of the unpredictability of his or her parents, the child learns that letting down the guard results in real pain...both emotional and physical. Normal "age-appropriate" childhood behaviors are often just not tolerated by parents who are either drunk or hung-over. Children need tons of love and attention. Children need nurturing, patience, tolerance and loving discipline that is consistent. None of these are available in an alcoholic household.   Due to pain of all sorts the child learns to constantly survey the environment on the look-out for conflict. When the child sees the conflict coming, behavior is modified to conform to the whims of the totally unpredictable alcoholic parent(s). At this point the child loses the most precious commodities of all...childhood wonder and spontaneity.

The truth is that none of the players in the lives of an addicted family are actually present. Even during those rare happy moments when some crises is not happening, looming or just happened, the family members are not present *as themselves*. How can they be when nobody really knows who they are in the first place? Everybody is playing a role written and directed by the addiction disease. But there are losses beyond childhood losses. What of the husband trying to support his family while keeping an alcoholic wife happy? She is dosing herself with her favorite flavor of a powerful depressant every few hours while he plays the enabler. He cleans up her messes; calls her boss to make excuses when she cannot make it to work (again) and he assumes an ever-larger role in performing the household duties.

Here is a question to ponder. While this husband is doing all of this, is he present for his children? Is he present for his neighbors, for his parents or even for himself? The same questions could apply for the son or father of an addict.

All that has been written here so far describes the situation. Now we need to point the reader in a direction to find help with this situation. Please, if you relate to this, find yourself a 12 step program. When you get yourself to a meeting, you will soon realize that delivering your body to a 12 Step meeting you will bring your mind along to be impacted by others who understand your situation. If you do this simple thing you will never be alone again. There are others who have faced what you are facing with dignity and learned how to live a full and productive life in spite of the price being paid for another's addiction disease. Sooner or later, if you stay with a 12 step program, you will begin learning these silly little slogans. One of those will be **"ONE DAY AT A TIME"**. As a man, you will begin, slowly, to unlearn those sick behaviors that everybody drummed into you all of your life. Yes, you will have to begin to *feel*. However; feeling is normal, healthy human behavior…not the messy display of weakness that you imagined it during the "troubles" part of your life. Feelings will no longer have to be stuffed or covered up with your own favorite addictions. You will learn to stop intellectualizing everything; to stop "figuring everything out" and to begin a whole new reality. As you step out into that scary place there will be benefits that had disappeared from the horizon for decades. You will even become present for the women and children in your life. Even better than all of that, *you will have a life!*

What do you want?

Codependent men often respond to this question with confusion, doubt and sometimes out and out anger! This is because we honestly do not *know* what we want. There is no question that, having lived with addicted loved-ones, we are living with a host of unmet wants and needs. However, they are more than unmet. They have not even been acknowledged by anybody else. Much worse, they have not been acknowledged by us *to* ourselves. One of the most important steps in spiritual recovery is to actually name our own wants and needs.

The good news is that this involves behavior and attitude and both of these can be changed. By now we have identified the fact that we are perpetually frustrated. We are racked with obsessions because we have been frantically trying to find some sort of relief for the frustrations caused by unmet needs. Maybe every man's deep need for sexual fulfillment, for example, has led to obsessive behaviors like addiction to pornography or an overactive fantasy life involving unavailable women around us every day. Maybe we are grossly overweight because we have tried to fill this vague but gaping hole in us with the gratification that comes from eating foods high in sugar and fat. Here is the supreme irony. Now that this situation has been brought to our consciousness, the answer to correcting it lies in our totally letting go of it.

Woman's Perspective on Expectations and the Dream Life

In order to see relief in loving, living with or knowing an addict is to simply let go of every notion, dream, expectation and desire involving the addict. We have to give up on the dream of how things should be in our lives because dreams create expectations that involve someone who is unable to fulfill our perceived role they must take within the dream. Expecting someone to be a certain person or fulfill a certain role in our lives is at the heart of frustration. It is this simple; if there is no expectation that any given desire or dream will be fulfilled by someone other than ourselves then there is no frustration experienced when our own imposed expectations are not met by the addict. The addict is not capable of fulfilling our own expectations; we must do those ourselves. If we want a better life, it must be sought after through our own steps in life and not of those around us. Those steps involve seeing your role in your own life and how to better yourself through help from a recovery program. Dreams are a necessary step in life but seeing the reality within those dreams is very difficult for someone who has lived with an addict. Our dreams are shattered and we feel a great loss associated with anger toward the addict. Our dreams become a part of a death in our lives. It becomes a grieving process because neither the "knight in shining armor" nor the "beautiful princess" is reality. The reality is that the addict will never be a part of the dream. The addict is a part of the reality. Once you are able to accept the fact that they control their own destiny; are you free to see your life healing through recovery.

Heard at a meeting. "God will give you what you need right at the moment when you need it."

Letting Go of the Dream Life and Seeing the New Path

Here is an exercise that may start a man on the path to accomplishing this process of releasing expectations. Try describing the unmet want or need out loud by yourself and then say again, out loud, so that your ears can hear the new attitude, "I don't even *want* this!" Drive this concept deeply into yourself. Take a clue from Clark Gable when he uttered the most famous line in Gone with the Wind... "frankly my dear; I don't give a damn." I really don't care if I get this or not. I have lived without this for years and I can live without it forever if it comes right down to it! It was when Clark Gable stopped chasing his love that she reversed roles and began to pursue him. Ultimately, only God can fulfill our deep spiritual needs but God cannot fill our souls when they are already tightly filled with frustration. We are all like little boys trying to get every jellybean we can possibly get out of a jar while grasping too many at a time. Let go of all of them, gentlemen, and you are well on your way to having them all. On a spiritual level, you will start to live again!

Men, ask yourself this question; how long has it been since you totally "lost it" to laughter? Do you sometimes go an entire day without laughing...a week? Laughter feels good. Laughter comes from a spirit that is light and free. Why don't we laugh more? Is it because laughter requires some loss of control? Is it because you cannot laugh without being in the present? Is it because you just don't see anything to laugh about right now?

Husband's Perspective on What is Next in Recovery

Addiction suppresses laughter because it renders us heavy and dark inside. There is not space in a mind that is full of worry, fear, doubt, anger and every imaginable projection about what might happen next for lightness of spirit. Complexity is heavy; simplicity is light. Our slogan in Al-Anon, "keep it simple" is profound. Before recovery, when I had a conversation with somebody and the conversation left me going away confused, I assumed that they were just more intelligent than I. That often led to poor self-talk. Through the program, I have learned that confusion is an elevated state of consciousness. Confusion teaches me. If the confusion is truly a lack of understanding then it can lead to growth. It means that I am still teachable. It means that I am still a work in progress and that I have a personal challenge to rise to some deeper level of understanding of a subject.

I have also learned that complexity sometimes comes because the other individual *wants it that way*. Confusion can also be an internal barometer to identify manipulation or guile in another. I like being around people who are direct. People who are direct never leave you wondering about where you stand with them. People who are indirect are what I call high maintenance friends. They require a great deal of energy and focus from me. They have gotten so adept at manipulating others into giving that to them that they do it even while you are aware that they are doing it! People who are deliberately complicated may have underlying messages such as "I am smarter than you are," or "I want you to feel sorry for my situation."

People who are wired inside to manipulate have some sort of an agenda with every topic. If you tell them with excitement that you are going to buy a new car tomorrow, they might answer with a subtle reference to the one they drive that is obviously more expensive than the one you are buying. Or maybe they start the conversation feigning an interest in you with a question such as "...how is your business doing?" Then, after you get out only one sentence, they launch into a long sad story about how they were just fired unfairly by a boss who was an ogre. You were set up to become their audience.

Passing judgment is heavy, whether we are condemning somebody else or ourselves. The internal beating that we give ourselves for who we are is called *shame* and the internal beating for our behavior is called *guilt*. Large books have been written on both of these subjects and none of the authors have anything good to say about either.

At one time I rationalized worry about a given topic as "thinking it through." The program has taught me the difference. If I consider many options; reason it out with other trusted people and then make a decision; that is thinking it through. If I pass the same vexing thoughts around and around tightly in my own head; exaggerate negative outcomes into future catastrophes and keep my thoughts a secret; then that is worry.

Let's move from spontaneous laughter to the broader subject… happiness. I once saw a carved sign in a gift shop that read:

"…if Momma ain't happy; ain't nobody happy."

If Momma doses herself with a powerful known depressant like alcohol every few hours throughout the day and night for years, "ain't nobody happy either!" Codependent family members face the almost dauntingly impossible task of proving the wisdom of that sign wrong. For example, I had to learn through recovery that I could laugh out loud while looking into the sullen bloated face of an angry inebriated wife. I had to learn that I could still enjoy hot apple pie with cheese and a strong cup of coffee while she glared at me across the table. These things were not easy but, after investing time and energy in learning detachment, I could do it!

The opposite of detachment (attachment) can be so absolute that the attached person even takes on the emotions of the addict. First, the codependent has perfected denial to the point where they are not only denying the pain they feel because of the diseased person's behavior; they have cut off feeling altogether! Happiness is out of the question first because it is a feeling and it has been erased with all of the others. If you don't know what happiness is; if you don't know what you feel; then the closest you are able to come to happiness might be the absence of pain. So here is your personal test; are you happy? If so, what causes that for you?

For the sake of understanding happiness, begin by digging into the issue. In the '60's we were all trying to "get it together ". What did that mean? As a child of the '60's I'll give my interpretation. Getting it together meant to be OK inside of you. It meant that you were living the way you thought you should be living and that your behavior matched your belief system. In today's AA vernacular, it meant that you walked like you talked.

When I seriously began working the steps I started "getting it together". I examined myself carefully with a loving sponsor (step 4) and then a knowledgeable priest (step 5). Through this process I learned exactly what I believe. I even learned that I have some values…that there are a few things that even I won't do. Below is what we call the Symptoms of Spiritual Awakening. While they may look different for each person, they still have the same theme:

12 SYMPTOMS OF A SPIRITUAL AWAKENING

1. An increased tendency to let things happen rather than make them happen.
2. Frequent attacks of smiling.
3. Feelings of being connected with others and nature.
4. Frequent overwhelming episodes of appreciation.
5. A tendency to think and act spontaneously rather than from fears based on past experience.
6. An unmistakable ability to enjoy each moment.
7. A loss of ability to worry.
8. A loss of interest in conflict.
9. A loss of interest in interpreting the actions of others.
10. A loss of interest in judging others.
11. A loss of interest in judging self.
12. Gaining the ability to love without expecting anything in return.

Heard at a meeting: "If I'm stuck in the past or the future, there is no point in praying for anything because I won't be present to receive it!"

PART III.
OUR STORIES

Son's Perspective: My mother was an alcoholic.

My secrets; my own brush with addiction, and finding Al-Anon. As dependent children, we had no escape and we naively believed that our families reflected the entire world; a world that seemed dangerous and unpredictable." <u>From Survival to Recovery,</u> P. #16. I noticed that the people at the meetings I attended who seemed the most like me identified themselves as adult children of alcoholics, so I began attending Al-Anon meetings that focused on adult children though at the time I couldn't imagine who in my family was an alcoholic. There I began to regain a sense of personal identity I hadn't realized was lost.

One morning, early in recovery, I stood in my bathroom staring at a perfect stranger in the mirror. Large blue eyes stared back at me from an expressionless face. Looking into my own eyes, I plunged into a bottomless river of sadness. I wanted to escape the sadness, but it was too late; I had begun to notice myself. Shocked, I recoiled and hurried off to work.

In the car, I noticed I maneuvered through the traffic like a soldier at war. At work, I saw that I functioned more like a machine than a man. Oh, I knew when to laugh, and when to be serious and when to elicit co-workers' confidences. But I shared none. Like a calculated chameleon, I hid well from any real human contact and I was desperately lonely.

At home, the mirror showed me a man who had hidden from himself and the world so effectively that he was a complete mystery even to himself. To solve the mystery, I had only the impetus of the great sadness, the loving support of new friends in the program, and the Twelve Steps of Al-Anon.

To find the man I needed to reclaim the child but I had no memories of my childhood. To defend myself against the intolerable pain of growing up in an alcoholic family I had buried all emotions and forgotten everything that happened as soon as it was over. Now I *couldn't* remember and my family *wouldn't*. For the barest outline of my life, I had to dig hard. Apparently, after I was born, I came to live with my grandmother straight from the hospital because my alcoholic mother, who already had a violent husband and two boys, refused to take me home.

The older I got, the less I thought of myself. Not being sure of myself was deadly on the playground. Local bullies made me their favorite target. Finally I made a friend who was funny and popular. As long as I hung around him, I didn't have to worry about being alone or attacked. He made many jokes at my expense and some of them hurt a lot but I was willing to pay *any* price to be included.

Paradoxically, while I took care of everyone who would let me; I tried to be completely self-sufficient. I was the "motor home man"; completely self-contained. Ever vigilant of my "friends", I waited for them to let me down. They usually obliged and then I redoubled my efforts at self-sufficiency. The repeating cycle of caretaking and emotional starvation lead to the desperate tears of my first night in Al-Anon.

The cycle begins as this: I was born into a family that had been battling the demons of alcohol, abuse and depression for many generations. The possibilities of an error in my memories surfaced after my mother's funeral in 1994. I was helping my father go through my mother's clothes and personal belongings. We were sorting the items into piles of what to keep and what to donate to charity.

The middle drawer of the dark wood dressers was my mom's safe.

Here she had deposited, between her hose and undergarments, her important documents. I opened the drawer and my nose caught a slight whiff of my mom's perfume mixed with the smells of wood and nylon. I reached in and pulled out a small box; my mom's safe. The box I had seen my mother often look through but was off limits to me like the play-boy magazine in my father's drawer. In this box were black and white photos of my mother when she was 17. Oh how beautiful & young looking she was. There were various photos of people I had never seen before and a marriage license.

The marriage license was for my mother and father and was issued on Jan. 5, 1968 in Delray Beach Florida. I was shocked by the date. They were married 2 weeks before I was born and I had always been lead to believe that they were married for year before I was born. The secret was out. The fantasy had taken a blow. I turned to my father. He shrugged his shoulders, a little embarrassed, and remarked; "we tried so hard to keep that a secret." I shrugged my shoulders and said it was no big deal.

However, it was a momentous occasion. It was the first blow to the wall of denial. If this belief was false, what else about my memories was false? Unfortunately, I was not ready to pursue the truth about my past just yet. I still wanted to hang out on the bank of familiarity even if it was false.

Family secrets are your secrets; your secret history. They are often not understood or known; yet they cause havoc in your life. It is the beginning; the initial step; the silence before the action. This is always an anxious and difficult time. The thoughts of "Am I good enough, smart enough or talented enough to begin and finish the task" swell in my conscious while fear spreads through my body temporarily paralyzing all thought or motion. Left unchecked these irrational thoughts roll like a dense fog over the dim flicker of rational thoughts. Insecurity pushes forward; smothering the sunshine rays of hope and possibilities. These are the thoughts that occurred when approached about the project of a men's Al-Anon book. One more was would my story really be worth listening to and would it be interesting? We will wait to find out.

The morning is gloomy, offering no hope of reprieve. Only the ever-present feeling of unhappiness and frustration remains. "How come I am miserable?" slides through my mind as my father-in-law tells me that *my unhappiness is a product of my thinking, which is a product of my past and for me to solve this I have to untwist the twisted past and resolve the issues to experience happiness.* I respond with an emphatic "I don't love your daughter and I made a mistake marrying her. That is the cause of my unhappiness; not my childhood past. I am leaving her for another woman who can make me happy. She understands me and can give me the things that your daughter can't. Don't talk to me about what I need to unwind to find happiness when what I need to do is undo my marriage to your daughter."

My first affair should have been a warning sign that there was a fault line running along my thinking. However, rather than conduct any introspection, I rationalized that my wife had made me into the adulterer and that I was justified in moving on even if this hurt my wife in the process. Selfishness was the route that I had chosen; all that mattered to me was my happiness and I could use and abuse anyone or anything in the effort to obtain it.

The affair did not last. No matter how many times I told myself that I was unhappy or told my wife that she caused me to seek an adulterous relationship I could not escape the words my father-in-law spoke to me. I indeed was unhappy; I had always been unhappy and I had convinced myself that I would one day be happy if I was successful, well regarded and financial well off. I chose to end the affair and attempt to restore my marriage. My wife got a small apartment while I went to live with my father.

My early attendance to a twelve-step program should have been the first sign that there was a fault line buried in the depth of my thinking. I was in the eighth grade and I had agreed with my parents to attend the Palmer Drug Abuse Program (PDAP). This agreement resulted from my mother discovering me in my room dividing pills for my friends into small bags at my desk. My mom's discovery turned the chaos filled house into even more turmoil.

I was an unhappy child with a positive attitude. I was shy yet out going; I was intelligent but played dumb; I was ambitious but indifferent and I was brave yet fearful and trusting yet doubtful. In short I was a chameleon with my feelings. I suffered without knowing I suffered because the acknowledgement of suffering would be too much because there was no hope of anything different.

My attendance at PDAP let me see the results of drug addiction first hand. In my meetings I discovered that I did not want to be a drug addict. I wanted something better. My sponsor, a young married lawyer, was fighting an addiction to cocaine. He was going to lose his law license and probably his wife due to a conviction of possession of cocaine with the intent to sell. I did not want my life to turn out that way. I wanted to be rich, successful and famous. I was convinced that this would be difficult to pull off if I was an addict and therefore made the decision not use drugs in the future. The fear of drug addiction and its consequences motivated me to pursue other avenues of relief from my unhappiness. These were sex, popularity, athleticism, idealism and materialism. The things that society deemed appropriate. During my involvement at PDAP I never discussed the reason for my unhappiness because I was unaware of the unhappiness. It would take another 21 years; two affairs; counseling and termination from a company that I had been employed with for 18 years before I would admit that there might be something wrong with me and sought help. What follows is the story of growing up in an alcoholic home; the effects this had on my thinking, on my choices, on my actions and the process I have gone through to reclaim my life.

I enjoy reading articles, viewing pictures and visiting archeological sites. The discovery of an ancient shard of a broken ceramic pot found on the ground, leads to a dig to unearth the past. The excavation, the marked off areas, and channels dug in the earth, all produced to answer the questions of what happened here, who lived here, how they lived and what caused their demise? The archeologist patiently reconstructs the past through the unearthing of artifacts and remnants of a history that has been covered by the debris of time. The redis-covery of my past has been a patient and painful process. Much like that of an archeologist, the journey into my past resulted from the dis-covery of broken shards of memories jutting up in my consciousness, like ancient ceramic shards, giving evidence to a troubled yet much covered and forgotten past. These memory pieces were unearthed through attending Al-Anon meetings, reading literature and talking with other Al-Anon's; especially the Al-Anon men.

My mother-in-law introduced me to Al Anon shortly after I had my first affair. She and my father–in-law thought that my actions of an affair were abnormal behavior (rightly so) however I believed that I was justified to seek happiness wherever or with whomever I thought might provide it.

Fear, the type that pulls your thoughts quickly past your heart to rest in your stomach overcomes me. I am being tossed to and fro in the driving seat of a covered wagon which is racing uphill. A glance to my right reveals a cowboy wearing tan leather chaps, a red ban-danna, a blue denim shirt and a taupe cowboy hat rounded at the top. In between us is a rifle, a Smith & Wesson with an oversize cock handle and dark mahogany wood stock. The cowboy says, "Keep your head down so;, them Indians are gaining on us", as he places his muscular left arm across my lap in an attempt to secure me. "What Indians?" I scream, as I turn my head to the left, extend my neck out like a turkey, peer over my shoulder and around the white canvas cover of the wagon.

Endless undulating hills covered in brown plains grass are re-vealed. I spot a thin column of smoke rising above the crest of a far off hill. The smoke is rising into the sky, pulsing to the beat of Indian drums and chanting. Bahm, Bahm, Bahm. Wah, Wah, Wah....

No matter how fast the horses draw the wagon forward over the country side the Indians, their smoke and chanting, continue to gain on us. I pick up the rifle; the coldness of the handle grabs my at-tention for a second. I turn; cock and point the rifle in the general direction of the Indians and fire. Hitting nothing, I manage only to increase their frenzied chase. They are gaining on us; I realize that they will catch us and scalp me and leave me to die. I imagine how badly it will hurt. We are doomed; hopeless!! Our efforts are futile we are caught and are merely extending the inevitable conclusion; our demise.

Suddenly I wake and realize it is only a dream. I am safe except I have wet the bed. This is no dream. I am hopeless. I will be punished for this. My mother will think I have done this on purpose. I am scared. I may get beat or yelled at or worse I'll be called a problem child.

The Story of MJR: A Fellow Mute Coyote

I drank and partied a lot as a young adult. I had a lot of social anxiety; fear of people and what they might think of me. Using alcohol and other drugs helped me feel more comfortable in social situations. At the age of thirty I was dating a woman who wanted to marry me; that was a new experience and flattering. We talked about having children, which wasn't my top priority but I felt ready to make a change in my life and looked forward to our life together.

My wife's drinking wasn't a problem to me at first but I had a big problem with my expectations regarding her behavior. As an artist, my income was typically modest and I'd warned her before we got married that I didn't earn enough money to support both of us. She said she would get a job. In the first few months of marriage we spent way more than I earned and my savings disappeared. I thought that when the savings ran out she would be forced to get work. She surprised me instead. She begged, whined and grumbled till I agreed to work more hours so she wouldn't have to get a job. The way she remembers it is that as soon as we got married I abandoned her so I could do what I really want to; which was work, and ignore her.

I was perpetually miserable. I complained about her unreasonable demands and expectations; the way she didn't care that I was suffering. I fantasized about leaving her; threatened to do that. I would come up with the most ridiculous reasons why I couldn't leave her: a deadline at work I couldn't miss, no one would feed the cats if I left. One night at a party we were both complaining loudly about each other. "How long does she think I will put up with her shit?" I said. My friend said "How long has it been so far?" I knew then that I was lost but what should I do about it? I only knew that complaining didn't help so I tried to stop doing that.

What did I get out of this sick relationship? Why couldn't I step out the door and just not come back? Part of the answer is that being a part of a couple brought me into the social group with other couples. I could look more normal. I had more in common with my friends because most of us were married. I could be a martyr and say "you wouldn't believe what she did this time". She had family in the area to visit on holidays and I didn't. Even sadder is the thought that maybe being miserable with her was a little better than being miserable by myself with no one to blame but myself.

After four years, I finally got the courage to tell her that I hated her and wanted a divorce. I was pleased to hear that she hated me, too, and wanted a divorce, too. A few minutes later she started pleading, apologizing and promising; talking about making a good relationship with me,\ and having a baby, because her doctor had said it should be now or never; with her medical history. Where did my resolve go? A couple of weeks later she got a plus sign on the home pregnancy test and told me to go make more money. I wasn't unhappy. I expected a lot of warmth, love and appreciation as we started this journey into parenthood. I couldn't have been more wrong. She was complaining, unhappy with my income; massages were no good; the food I prepared for her tasted like shit. I felt betrayed and leaving her wasn't something I felt I could do; not when she was pregnant or with a baby or toddler or school age child.

Of course I loved and enjoyed my daughter; she loved me and gave my life an undeniable legitimate purpose. My wife was critical and unhappy with me and our life in general. Two months after our daughter was born my wife announced that she needed a break every afternoon. I worked at home and had already agreed that I would help a lot with the baby so I started spending two to four hours each afternoon cooking, cleaning and playing with our baby. I worked evenings to make up for the lost work day hours. For some reason my wife had started drinking wine after her morning coffee; a lot of it. She became even angrier and verbally abusive toward me. I kept trying to appease her and keep up with her demands. Years later I would check up on her at 2:45 each afternoon to see if she was awake to get our daughter from grade school. Sometimes I couldn't wake her up and picked up our daughter myself. Sometimes she would be angry at me for checking up on her; other times, appreciative.

> Heard at a meeting: "If I feel uncomfortable in a situation maybe it's not me. Maybe it's my Higher Power saying to me that there is somebody I don't trust here and maybe I shouldn't!"

My world was shrinking. I lived and worked by myself at home; once a week I would go to the city in the afternoon to pick up and deliver work. That was all the social life I had. My mother was so upset at the language and the way my wife treated me that my parents refused to visit us ever again. Years earlier, after getting home from parties, she'd complained so bitterly about my talking to women that I quit talking to any women at parties, married or single, in an effort to appease her. Then she wanted me to stop going to the bar or parties; none of our friends met her standards any more. In an effort to have some relationship with her I would pick a couple of articles of interest in the newspaper and tell her about them; try to get a discussion going. She got bored with that and criticized and put me down till I stopped reading the newspaper at all. She even decided she didn't like me eating fruit preserves on my toast and picked at me till I gave that up as well. I really had nothing left to give up for her.

I was depressed and really wanted away from her. I didn't want to leave my daughter but the hostility and threats were so unrelenting, I couldn't imagine staying. I made an elaborate plan to escape and for the first time actually started to leave forever not just for a night as a threat. I needed a few weeks without work to move and set up shop elsewhere. I told most of my customers that I needed to catch up on work for the others. That story wasn't going to work with one client who I did have an especially good relationship with. I decided to tell the truth about leaving my family, I started talking about my wife's drinking all day every day and the verbal abuse and anger. My client stopped me and started telling me about Al-Anon and Al-a-teen and Alcoholics Anonymous. My client had a long history in AA that I'd been unaware of and we talked for about an hour about the benefits of Al-Anon for me and how my wife and daughter might be helped as well. It had never occurred to me to look for help independent of my wife.

I decided to put my plan to escape the marriage away and try to change my wife instead. That makes me laugh now. I knew she wouldn't stop drinking if I was still drinking so I stopped. I wanted to start Al-Anon but I was overwhelmed with work so there was a two month delay. After six weeks she hadn't noticed that I wasn't drinking and I pointed it out to her to get some discussion started about sobriety. She thought sobriety was a good idea for me. I finally got to a couple of Al-Anon meetings. I felt supportive comfort in the company of others struggling with some of the same problems I had. I felt new hope that I could continue living with my family. I had hope that I could influence my wife to make her stop drinking. Al-Anon literature suggested to me that changing our own behavior may cause the alcoholic to seek treatment. I focused my attention on that idea; not paying attention to the one that says we can only change ourselves and are powerless over others.

I didn't explicitly ask my wife to change her behavior; I tried to make changes I wanted. I lost a lot of weight on a doctor recommended low cholesterol diet. She was violently opposed to the diet; apparently fearful of losing control over me. My attendance of Al-Anon groups was taken by her as personal criticism and violently resented. I tried to avoid arguing with her or seeing her at all. She drank more than ever and would argue vehemently with anyone with insults, put downs, and threats. When that became too much or got physical I would escape to the park or bookstore. She said I was undermining her parental authority and called the assistant principal at our daughter's school to insist that the girl be given a Saturday detention for being tardy once. Our daughter expressed a desire to run away or flunk her classes on purpose as a slap at her mother. My wife's hostility was expressed verbally and physically. At one point she said "This is not alcoholism, it is abuse. Why do you stay here and take it? What's wrong with you; you piece of shit" Good question. I wanted to live with my family; with my daughter and protect her. I was afraid of being alone and my wife threatened suicide whenever we discussed divorce.

I worked at home and was confronted, threatened and lectured by my angry wife pretty often. After one incident turned out violent, my feelings were badly hurt. I wanted justice and was determined to leave this time. I made a police report at the station but had cooled down a little and didn't press charges. I needed a car so I went and bought one that evening. The next morning she found me by phone at the motel. She was remorseful and said she would stop drinking and that she loved me and wanted us to have a good life together. I was relieved and excited that everything I wanted seemed to be ready to happen. I already had an appointment to meet my Al-Anon sponsor for breakfast so I did that before going home. He told me very gently that her behavior, the remorse and promises, were textbook alcoholic behaviors, and would probably not last long. I knew this was true. I'd heard other people's similar stories and read the AA big book and knew he was right.

She talked about going to AA until her hangover got better and then her bluster and hostility returned. She couldn't do AA because "they would talk about God." She said "put locks on your door if you're afraid of me" and "Al-Anon is a misogynistic cult." In just three days I had to leave the house again to get away from her. I still wasn't done trying to get her to stop drinking; I thought that would make me happy. I told her twice that I would leave her if she didn't stop drinking. I didn't get her attention. She said she would go to AA if I went, too, and stopped going to Al-Anon. I thought that would be worth it if it worked so I agreed. I was ready to go to the AA meeting; she was topping up her tumbler of wine. We never went to one meeting, I was discouraged and stopped my Al-Anon meetings even though she hadn't held up her part of the bargain.

For three more months we continued the way we always had. One beautiful fall day I went upstairs for breakfast and found my wife in a foul drunken mood. I spent all morning working and at lunchtime I was pleased to find her gone with her sister and our daughter. They were no doubt having lunch somewhere or shopping. I took the dogs for a walk. When I got back her sister and our daughter were sitting on the front porch, I said hello and went inside, hoping my wife was taking a nap. She was in the kitchen and laid into me verbally when I walked in. I left my food on the counter and headed for the stairs. She blocked my exit and we struggled all the way downstairs, past her sister and our daughter. I was holding her wrists to keep her from hitting me and she tried to bite my hand so I let her go and she punched me and split my lip. It was all over then and she went inside and I cleaned up and spent the rest of the day entertaining myself away from home. I was angry but I knew that if I wanted to live with my daughter, I had to put up with this behavior.

The next day her sister said she wanted to take our daughter away from both of us; out of our sick relationship. Finally I could see that we were harming our daughter and each other by staying together and I decided to leave immediately. This time I didn't threaten to leave I simply had a moving company show up and take my office away. I didn't want to be talked out of this again. I'd started Al-Anon almost a year earlier to try and change my wife's behavior. I'm back now to change my own behavior; to figure out what I want in life and go get it and stop feeling responsible for making my wife's life what she wanted. That is *her* responsibility; not *mine*. I need to know what I got out of being a martyr and victim and find healthy ways to relate to others. I need to learn about myself enough to recognize my dysfunctional behavior in relationships to avoid repeating the same patterns with new partners.

Husband's Perspective on Patterns

I would like to summarize my 19 year marriage to an alcoholic wife with a quote from the September 26th reading in our daily reader, Hope for Today;

> *"I wanted to create a perfect family and that was all. At 20 years old, the idea didn't seem crazy. My parents had divorced and I wanted to prove I could do marriage differently so I married someone who needed me. At our wedding ceremony, the minister said "and the two shall become as one," and we did.* ***WE BECAME HER.***

In my case, Mom was perfectly sober but she was more than likely wringing her hands over the latest crisis involving the members of *her* family just down the street. Grandma kept her and Dad up all night last night because she got drunk rolled over between the bed and the wall and Grandpa called in a panic because she was so heavy that he couldn't get her un-stuck. That may sound funny, but when it's *your* mother (or grandmother) it just doesn't work with the standard Hallmark card version of a Grandmother! Unfortunately, the cure for being drunk during the 50's was a cold shower so here you had three grimly knowing adults who had to undress this woman completely and maneuver her, stark naked as she railed against them, into a cold shower. Can you imagine what that looked like? Grandma was less than 5' tall, and she weighed over 200 pounds!

Meanwhile, as Grandma sleeps it off, life has to go on, and Dad has to get up early and go to work on the construction crew. Or maybe Dad is missing altogether. He is out flying airliners; leading his sales team; saving a corporation; writing a sermon or healing the sick. Dad is holding everything together because that is the way *he* learned a real man functions.

I was living with a role model who demonstrated how "real men" behave. Real men face life with resolution; buck up; get up; get going and get to work. Real men never confront for fear of embarrassment, either for themselves or for the members of their families. Real men never complain because they are just made of better stuff than that. Real men hold down a full time job, bust their asses nights and weekends to build rent-houses bare-handed from the ground up using nothing but hand tools and they have to win every game or contest they enter. But they never gripe, they never brag, *and they never take any credit*. This is because real men are…well, real men.

My Dad and Henry Fonda were both 17 when Mr. Fonda was starring in the movie "Grapes of Wrath," except that Mr. Fonda was in *front* of the camera and Dad was working as a scab laborer for the movie company carrying equipment. They had picked up Dad on the streets of Bakersfield when they asked him "…do you know where the Okies are?" He had just arrived from Arkansas on his own the second time as a youngster trying to escape the ravages of poverty and alcoholism. His Mom had drunk and caroused in a small Arkansas town where everybody knew everybody and this was at a time when that was really considered bad. On at least one occasion he had lived through her attempted suicide by downing an entire fifth of vodka. He knew shame. Shortly after the time of the stock market crash of '29, Dad, at about the age of twelve, had already tried to escape by walking and hitch-hiking east to Florida with one of his buddies. They had made a harrowing adventure but had to return to their squalid existences at home after almost starving to death.

I still cannot watch The Grapes of Wrath without crying because now I understand the truth after all of these years. Henry Fonda and the other actors in the movie were playing the roles of a heroic family struggling against the hardest times America had ever known but Dad and Mom weren't acting. They were the real thing!

Mom, now in her 80's, tells me they were not really called "Okies" in 1937. That may have been helped along by "Hollywood." They were called "fruit tramps." With either slight, it was not an easy way to maintain "self esteem," (or survive). Her family, exactly like Dad's, had functioned under the heavy weight of *shame*.

There was, however, always the escape of alcohol. Mom's oldest and youngest brothers both died of the disease, the oldest, even in 1962, had "Cause of death, <u>acute alcoholism</u>" written on his death certificate. That was highly unusual in the early '60's. Both of these men lived a half block away from us at various times throughout my childhood; they both died living in the same little house; they both drank on the same old couch. As a boy child with an untreated Al-Anon Dad, what kind of modeling does this little boy witness day in and day out? Men are caretakers. Men do not themselves need attention. So who does this hero child grow up and marry?

A perfect is example of the hero child as a grown married man would be as follows:

We arrived on a Sunday afternoon and shortly after we checked into our hotel room one of those horrific summer plains area thunder storms hit. I had just received a major promotion from my company. I was to become a hospital specialist, focusing on sales and marketing in a group of major medical centers. Being from San Diego, we had never experienced anything like this. It was dark outside and the "boomers" were shaking the windows. My wife wanted a drink. I went downstairs to buy it for her but was told that, because of the "Blue Laws," alcohol could not be legally sold on Sundays. This would just not do and I KNEW IT. Deb had to have her drink, and I knew that if I didn't come back with it, well, there would just be hell to pay.

I took this bellman off to the side, handed him a twenty dollar bill, and told him something like '…you find a way to open that locked door to that little liquor cabinet back there and get me a bottle of vodka.' He did exactly that and the crisis was averted. As we sat and drank, we agreed that this state was an awful place.

Husband's Perspective: Facing Her with My Program

The male Al-Anon, if he ever does manage to haul himself to a meeting, is faced with a simple Program that obviously works. The whole process has to start with the first step, which begins with those very words of surrender that he just cannot accept!

I must have really looked like the "deer in the headlights" as I sneaked into my first Al-Anon meeting in the little upstairs room at an AA club one night in Dallas, 300 miles from my home. I was there; not so much because I was seeking growth or recovery; I didn't even have those notions available at that point in my mind. I was there because, after one horrible night in my living room at home, I had surrendered and found the Al-Anon office in Atlanta. There God arranged for my first sponsor, Scotty L., to walk into the room. It was Scotty who just stayed after me to attend a meeting. I owe him so much today. They were all women; they were all older than I and I knew none of them. I was out the back door without a word to anybody that night. I remember nothing; felt overwhelmed and sneaky at furtively going to this meeting while away from home. I worried about betraying my wife and, most of all, I feared the emotional pain I knew that she would cause me if she ever found out that I had told ANYBODY about her drinking. Thank God, the years and the program have been kind. I no longer have to live with active alcohol consumption in my home and, because of the Al-Anon program, I am surrounded by love every day!

Even if he overcomes these internal pressures, the man with the alcoholic wife faces another set. Immediately upon learning of this thing called Al-Anon, the alcoholic wife attacks it. She calls it a cult; she mocks it. Later, if she learns enough of the Program vocabulary, she will use it to hammer him.

"I thought you were supposed to be detached..."

Here is what happened when I finally admitted to my wife that I was attending Al-Anon meetings. In early 1976, after months of sneaking around, my sponsor would no longer accept my excuses. He knew that just one meeting attended in a small town 300 miles away "on the sly" was not enough to work this program!

So he pinned me down on the phone one Thursday afternoon. He said that I needed to go to a meeting. He told me that there was a meeting that night at Doctor's Hospital. I finally made the commitment to show up at 8:00 and meet him at Doctor's Hospital. When I hung up the telephone I felt a hole in the pit of my stomach. I would have to somehow do this and then I would have to admit to my wife that Al-Anon existed; that I had found it and that I had 'joined'.

What happened next is an illustration of how a male Al-Anon functions in his dysfunctional family on a daily basis. Notice as you read this that I was by now taking care of the greater part of the household and parenting duties. The first person to stroll through the door after school that day was Raymond, my oldest son. He off-handedly, over his shoulder, informed me that I was taking him and one of his buddies to Central Park Amusement Center. I was to take them right away. I told him that I couldn't do that because I couldn't pick them up later, as I had a meeting to attend at 8:00. He flew into a rage saying:

"...what do you mean, you have a meeting? I already told this guy that my Dad would drive us!" He stomped out of the kitchen.

Then his younger brother came in from school. He asked, again, matter-of-factly:

"What's for dinner?"

I told him that I didn't know, and that I had to leave at 7:00 for a meeting. He was confused:

"A meeting? What kind of a meeting and who is going to make dinner?"

I went to the meeting and it was a very eventful evening. As a newcomer (remember, this was only my second meeting after the one out of town) I was all ears. I don't even remember anything said at that meeting but something happened after the meeting that I will never forget. After the meeting, one of the two other men in attendance approached me and started talking. I had no idea who he was or what his situation was. Little did I realize that God was using me for His purposes; even during my second meeting! After he walked away Barry, my sponsor, walked up and asked me something like this;

"What did he say?"

I just relayed a few remarks, none of which I felt were significant. My sponsor then told me this:

"Did you read in the paper yesterday about the woman who jumped from the twenty- something floor of the Hilton Hotel downtown and landed on a Grand piano in the lobby?"

I said,

"...no, I didn't read it."

My sponsor said,

"...well, that was her husband."

My sponsor told me that this guy had attended meetings for a while and that, since there were only a handful of men in Al-Anon in the city, the guy was pretty well known. Looking back on this now, I see this as ironic. Of all those people in that room, I was probably the only one who didn't know about this man's situation and yet he approached me. I had no knowledge of miracles then; I had no faith and almost no spirituality. A nuance that escaped me at the time but that I can see now as an experienced Al-Anon, is that this man was 12-stepping *me* as a "newcomer." He approached me to encourage me. Working his program in true fashion, even given the extraordinary circumstances of his own life, he told me to "Keep coming back!"

My sponsor said the funeral was to be soon and that a lot of program people would be attending. He asked me if I wanted to go but I was already trying to imagine the price I would pay for being out at this meeting. My head was on what would happen when I came home. Telling Deb that I was going to a funeral for another alcoholic woman who had committed suicide was just beyond my imagination! I had a great deal to think about as I drove home but the moment I walked through the door from the garage into the den I was attacked by my wife.

"Where the Hell have you been?" "Do you realize that I had to walk home from work?"

She had gotten another tech job at a nearby hospital. It was two blocks away from our house.

"By the time I had walked home it was after 7:00 and these kids hadn't even been fed yet...where were you?"

I told her.

That was the night. It was another night of fighting as she drank. It went on and on. I would try to go to bed but she would follow me down the hall disparaging me in every way she could imagine. Like so many times before, I just wanted to get away.

Heard at a meeting: "I slip fast when I don't get around y'all."

Husband's Perspective: The Car Wars.

After I attended my first meeting in a new town, my wife became aware that I was attending weekly meetings. We began the period I remember as the "car wars." I got an Al-Anon schedule and found out that there was a Friday night meeting at that hospital only a couple of miles from where we lived. We had only one car at that time...my company car. My wife would simply take our car shopping on Friday nights and not come home until well after 9:00. The meetings were from 8:00-9:00 so that took care of that. I caught on the first time she pulled this and just walked to the meeting that night. As usual, this infuriated her and that weekend was a long one. Even at this early point in my program I had experienced at least a small level of serenity and for the first time I refused to surrender that to her disease.

My final victory in the car wars came when I took advantage of my back yard mechanic skills. I just popped the hood on the company car earlier in the evening on the following Friday; took the cap off of the distributor (only two clips); pulled the rotary pin out and put it in my pocket. The first time I did this, she stormed into the living room yelling:

"...What did you do to the car?"

I told her I had fixed the car so that I could drive it any time I wanted and that she couldn't. The following week I again left for the Friday meeting after spending about two minutes under the hood, during which Deb stood in the doorway calling me everything but a Christian! Notice that I had been practicing the Program for more than four months before my wife actually asked about it. Trying to figure out why she was suddenly so interested in my program is impossible but from what I have learned working with other men in similar situations, my guess is she was seeing subtle changes in my behavior.

Yes, the program does work from the inside out and the change is permanent. Yes, sooner or later the personal growth leads to behavior change and, while the relationship between an alcoholic wife and a codependent husband is sick, it is still terribly close. She is accustomed to reading her Al-Anon husband easily and manipulating him is even easier. But, lately, when pushing one button doesn't work, the alcoholic has had to try pushing others. When pushing no button works, the alcoholic has to push...*harder*. Finally, when *nothing* works, the alcoholic gets curious. What is happening here?

Husband's Perspective on Finally Leaving

These are early feelings from my diary, written in 1982, in a supermarket coffee shop. So I'll just start writing in this log...a "feelings log," in the hopes the exercise will help pull me out of this morass of downness. How long has it been since I left my home, my marriage, my boys, my neighbors, that 'other life?' I left on Feb 20 at 11:00 PM just no longer willing to sacrifice my last few decades to an alcoholic wife. Yes, I know she is very sick; yes, I know she is powerless over the booze; yes, I know that the disease is progressive; that she will just get sicker from here on out. But I don't have the stuff it takes to stick it out to the finish.

I had somehow pictured myself with her all the way to the end... a kind of blind, sick, loving devotion to an ideal that never was... unconditional love. "I'll love you; I'll stay with you; I'll protect you and I'll be that 'Bridge over Troubled Waters'." But God showed me the end while at the old General Hospital downtown. As part of my continuing education as a pharmaceutical salesman covering the hospitals in a major medical center, my company had arranged for a kind of preceptor ship at a teaching hospital in downtown. I was to 'shadow" a third year internal medicine resident for two solid weeks. We had three reps assigned to each resident and that little group of four worked together day and night. We were in the ER overnight; in the clinics seeing patients all day across the street from the hospital and, of course, we had to make "rounds" every evening. We were rounding one night when the resident said:

"...would you like to see our yellow man?"

We all crowded into this small patient room. The resident began droning in that "rounds tone" that he had learned from so many of his professors.

"This is the last stage of acute alcoholism."

I was shocked at the bright yellow color of the man's skin. He was the color of an egg yolk! His liver shutdown had caused bilirubin to back up in his blood. In the resident's words,

"...bilirubin is liquid shit. It is the total of all of the debris from his intestines that has not been filtered through a functioning liver."

What I saw was the bloated belly, the NG tubes, IV lines, the academic detachment of the IM resident demonstrating the testicular atrophy, the elevated liver function values...SGOT, amylase or pancreas shutdown, the BUN...all numbers, letters, tubes, putrid smells. After he showed us the amazingly enlarged breasts under the gown, he said;

"...alcohol suppresses the naturally occurring male hormones that normally balance the female hormones. This results in an

exaggeration of the female secondary sex characteristics. You wind up with a guy with balls the size of grapes and boobs the size of melons"

We finally left the horrible little room. As we wondered down the hall toward the tiny family cubicle I saw my counterpart in the alcoholism drama; only a woman. There she was with her adult daughter. I stared into her eyes...*my eyes* someday and saw raw agony. She and her daughter were just standing off to the side waiting for him to die.

There was literally nobody there. After living with this man throughout the years while he drank himself to death, she had lost all feeling. I was reminded of those old zombie movies, where the dead walk through the night. Neither of us said a word but I saw another price paid by human beings suffering from the disease of alcoholism at that moment. I wonder what impact this man's disease has had to this day throughout his family...among people like his daughter. She said,

"...please let him go."

She was pleading with the resident. It was beyond tears. It was beyond questions. It was beyond anything I had imagined in my martyr daydream. It was a living hell being in her brain. At least he was unconscious.

Heard at a meeting: "Alcohol has been a reliever of pain for a long time. 1900 years before Christ the Egyptians were stupefying patients with tooth aches with alcohol before extracting an infected tooth!"

I had three years of Program under my belt at that point and it took me another three years of clinging to the dream. It took another three years of hard work in The Program with mile after mile going under my feet as I ran down the Bayou. This brings up another common characteristic of male Al-Anon's. Some of us are in amazingly good physical condition. When we discover exercise, it does more for us than for other men. Exercise is a release. Exercise is time away from the disease. Exercise adds an element of pleasure to our existence and it is perfectly acceptable to society. As a hero child and as a man who does not enjoy that much respect from other men exercise affords the male Al-Anon a strong attractive body. If he is truly working his program he has cleaned up his own act in terms of smoking, drinking and diet as well. Now he is getting regular check-ups, taking care of his teeth and getting more rest and relaxation…all of which eventually serves him well on a purely physical level. I remember the four-mile runs down the bayou. Somehow, I thought that if I could keep my body and mind together, to stay whole, to be so solid, to stay glued together myself, bit would somehow miraculously hold us both together. I thought it would hold our marriage together, ut my wife just kept dodging. She just kept climbing into her Ernest and Julio Gallo jug night after night instead of living. I still wonder:

"Why does she have to do that? What could possibly be God's motive for taking someone's life in such a horribly slow fashion?"

So I left.

I wish my story had a happy ending for everybody. Actually it did for me and for our sons but it didn't for Deb. Deb succumbed to her disease of substance abuse in April of 2010, just as this very book was in progress. She never knew it was being written.

Father's Perspective: My Daughter was an Addict

Before relating how this disease progressed through the four stages for my daughter and me, I believe it is important to discuss who we each were and what our relationship was like before the addiction process started. My daughter, from a very young age was a very sensitive, caring and trusting person. She loved all animals, was loyal to her friends and was always concerned about other people and their emotional and physical well being. She had an especially kind heart for the poor and would insist on helping them; often getting upset with me for not responding sufficiently. She also had a very high independent nature and, at this early age, often insisted on doing things herself and doing them her way. Of all her character traits, the one that stood out the most was her complete and absolute trust of everyone and a lack of any kind of boundaries in her relationships. As she approached her teen years, this trait proved to be the most damaging and caused a lot of hurt and pain. One example was when her best friend dropped her when her friend entered high school and my daughter was still in the eighth grade. She was devastated and did not seem to recover from this experience. I suspect there were many other situations where this trait caused hurt before her addiction started and I know there were many after it started which will be discussed later. Neither my daughter nor I knew at the time that she was genetically predisposed to the disease of addiction. There was addiction on both my side and her mother's side of the family. This predisposition along with the character trait of complete trust of others and the resulting hurt thus set the stage for using addictive substances to medicate the pain she experienced.

In addition to the stage being set by the two factors mentioned, she was also raised by an angry, controlling and resentment filled father. I was not aware of these traits when she was young and not until I attended Al Anon for several years did I recognize them and the damage they did to my daughter. My grandfather who lived in the home I grew up in was an alcoholic and my mother was an extreme codependent. My negative character traits developed as a defense mechanism to my home environment. It is important to point out here that I no longer feel any need to blame, feel anger, resentment or to be judgmental toward my mother or grandfather. I can now see clearly that they also suffered from the effects of the disease of addiction just like I did and my daughter did. Other character traits I had before my daughter's addiction started included a strong drive for achievement through education and in my business career. I also tended to avoid letting others get close to me and was not considered to be very approachable. The only emotion I knew I had was anger and it was expressed frequently and only I was allowed to express it within my family. These character traits of mine coupled with those of my daughter made for a difficult relationship for both of us.

The best way I can describe our relationship is that it was like the "irresistible force (me) and the immovable object (my daughter)". Looking back on this aspect of our relationship, I can now see that she was just like me. I absolutely rebelled against anyone who tried to tell me what to do and would in fact do just the opposite to prove the point that I think and act on my accord and not at the commands of others. I can remember a high school principal telling me that I was not college material and that I should pursue a trade. Five years later I received my MS degree in Chemical Engineering and realized I owed him a debt of gratitude. I told my daughter that a college education was a requirement in our family and not surprisingly, she decided not to get one. As her rebellious nature increased and my need to control remained, our relationship grew distant on the surface. Beneath this, however there was a deep love and respect that was not often expressed. What I do know now is that she had a strong need to be close to and spend time with her father but I was not able to provide it. I kept her at a distance because of fear that my approval would reinforce her rebellion and also because I had difficulty getting close to anyone at that time. Given our character traits, her inheritance of the addiction genetics and our relationship, we both moved into the disease process through the four stages mentioned earlier.

Stage 1 of the Downward Spiral

It is difficult to determine exactly when my daughter's addiction started. There was a change in her attitude, study habits and mood starting at around age 12 or 13. She seemed sad and withdrawn at times and started to exhibit low self esteem. Some of her friends exhibited the same traits while others seemed happy and normal. She had developed an interest in sports but abandoned these activities during her freshman year in high school. We found out later that she had used both alcohol and marijuana during this time period. During her second year in high school my job required a geographical relocation which was extremely difficult for her. She began acting out at school; her grades declined and her rebelliousness increased. At the same time, my efforts to control her and my fears about where she was headed increased. This fear was especially real for me when some weird boyfriends started showing up. She was now very attractive but was attracted to boys who were dropping out of school; were in trouble or were abusive toward her. I think her low self esteem coupled with a need to help or rescue others was what made these boys attractive to her. At about this time she started attending parties where alcohol and possibly drugs were available and seemed to live for them. She also started going to bars every weekend and seemed to look forward to the escape from her problems and especially from the difficult adjustment to the geographical move. I think this was the "happy" part of stage 1 for her because the alcohol and or drugs made the pain go away and were also finally something she could rely on to have "fun."

During this stage my efforts to control and protect her and my fears continued to increase. There were many arguments about her behavior, her boyfriends and all night parties. The preaching and lecturing was frequent and at times I raged at her. On one occasion she and her brother brought marijuana with them on a trip out of the state and could have been arrested for possession of illegal drugs. I raged at both of them for about 30 minutes pointing out what could have happened. My son more or less accepted the scolding but my daughter became even more rebellious – back to the irresistible force and the immovable object analogy. I know now that a better approach would have been to express my concern sternly but more calmly and to discipline them with love. At the time, I could only see the dreams I had for my children going down the drain and could not deal with the reality that their future was not going to work out the way I had envisioned. Because of my reactions and my daughter's increasing rebelliousness, our relationship continued to deteriorate. Also, my focus on my daughter and her behavior increased and I began to neglect my other children and their needs. The character traits I had before my daughter's addiction started were beginning to be amplified at this point and we were both beginning to move into stage two of the process.

Stage 2 of the Downward Spiral

During this stage there were both positive and negative directions that my daughter was taking. She enrolled in college on two different occasions but then dropped out and eloped at age 19. She became pregnant and had her first child at age 20. During her pregnancy, she enrolled in nursing school and graduated at the top of her class. She was focused on her degree and avoided alcohol for the most part during the pregnancy. The marriage did not work so she divorced and then gave full custody to her ex-husband. As it turned out giving up her son was probably an act of love on her part but was a source of grief and pain for the rest of her life. This "consequence" was one of the emotional pains which she continued to medicate with alcohol and drugs. She also began to isolate from the family and would not show up for holidays or other family events after giving up custody of her son. The use of alcohol increased and another boyfriend introduced her to hard drugs at about this time. Her denial started and she would say that everyone drinks and uses a few drugs including our neighbor.

During this second stage of the process, I continued to painfully watch the destructive path my beautiful daughter was taking. My focus on her increased and I started "helping" her with loans; moving to different apartments; buying cars and trying even harder to control her. I made phone calls to her boyfriend's parents and raged at them for not doing something about the alcohol and drug use. My frustration and anger increased and I started isolating from others and spent more and more time on my job. Shame also started to set in as friends and neighbors became aware of what was happening in our family. The image of the "perfect" family I had hoped for was crushed and now I had to acknowledge that my family was not even normal. I started to become aware of how judgmental society is about the disease of addiction and experienced strange looks and avoiding behaviors on the part of some my acquaintances (I now refer to them as acquaintances rather than friends). While there was clearly a judgmental attitude, I must accept that I also played a part by avoiding contact with others including relatives because of the shame I felt. I pushed people away at the very time in my life when I needed healthy relationships the most. This hiding or denial process started and continued into stage 3 for both my daughter and me.

Stage 3 of the Downward Spiral

Denial for my daughter was exhibited by continually running from the addiction with numerous job changes, boyfriends, marriages, and moving to new apartments. At the same time some serious losses began to occur. During a ten year period there were multiple job changes working as an RN, at least six moves to various apartments and five boyfriends. It seemed that each succeeding boyfriend was more abusive than the previous one. The abuse ranged from infidelity to severe physical and emotional abuse. All of them were also addicts using alcohol and hard drugs with her. She became pregnant with her second child during this time period and the father had an affair during her pregnancy. She then met an even more abusive man at an AA meeting. She had broken bones, severe bruises, was left at parties and other places without transportation home from this abusive man. Still, she denied that he was a threat to her emotional well being and her life saying that he had some very good qualities and that many of their arguments and fights were her fault. Her use of drugs and alcohol increased and at this point were used to medicate her feelings and the hurt she was experiencing rather than to have "fun" as was the case in an early stage in her life. I also believe that she was addicted to this abusive man and that her addiction to him was as powerful if not more powerful than her addiction to alcohol and drugs.

The denial that alcohol and drugs were the problem continued despite some serious consequences and losses that were occurring. She was arrested for cocaine position and spent time in jail for the first time. She also lost her RN license several times and was terminated from at least four jobs because of absenteeism. In addition, her parents intervened and obtained custody of her daughter at age 3 because she was actively using drugs while raising her. There were multiple car accidents and cars sold to drug dealers. She did make several attempts at recovery after some of these losses.

The recovery attempts involved a total of seven admissions to treatment centers with some of them being court enforced and others voluntary. Her periods of sobriety after these treatment center stays ranged from a few days to over a year on one occasion. In most cases after a day or two in treatment, she would deny that she needed help and that she already knew what she had to do to stay sober. The denial at this point was so strong that she completely blocked out of her mind what had just happened to her including the losses mentioned previously.

My denial during this stage involved the belief that I could do something about her addiction and her involvement with abusive men. I helped her move numerous times; bailed her out of jail; left her in jail; replaced wrecked cars; drove her to treatment centers; gave her a shoulder to cry on when she was in trouble and did many other things to get her sober. Nothing worked and in fact things continued to get worse after each attempt to "help". I became more and more obsessed with her problems and trying to help her and was not available to my sons. They did not have a father who was available for them to talk about their emotional needs and concerns. Also, they did not want to put additional burden on the family by talking about their issues and so learned to stuff their feelings. The effects of living with addiction were thereby passed along to them. Another problem for me was that I continued to avoid discussing what was happening to my daughter with extended family or with friends. I was basically isolated socially except for superficial relationships with co-workers and golfing buddies.

Heard at a meeting: "God doesn't have any grandchildren."

Later during this 10 year period I started attending Al-Anon meetings after learning about it during a family session at one of the treatment centers. I attended meetings weekly for about two years and then dropped out of the program deciding that it wasn't helping me. I learned later that I was not ready to admit my powerlessness over my daughter's addiction and thus had not been willing to embrace the spiritual foundation of the Al Anon program. Newcomers to the program are told that their misery will be refunded if they decide not to continue in the program. Mine was fully refunded as the disease progressed for both my daughter and me so I rejoined the program a few years later.

Stage 4 of the Downward Spiral

Even with numerous treatment center stays and short periods of recovery the severity of the relapses and the consequences for my daughter increased to the point where I now believed that she would not survive this disease. She began to overdose on cocaine and when hospitalized the first time was on a respirator when my wife and I went to the emergency room. Here was my beautiful daughter lying in a hospital bed, unresponsive and near death. It hit me hard for the first time that she may not survive and I totally lost it emotionally crying uncontrollably in the men's rest room. She survived this overdose but there would be many more overdoses, visits to jail and abuse by her boyfriend as well as periods of extended recovery time.

At this point both my daughter and I were in recovery programs. She was attending AA and NA meetings and I was attending Al-Anon meetings two to three times per week. She received a one year sobriety chip at an AA meeting which she asked me to attend with her. I remember the hope and pride I felt when she received the chip and also that she had grown tremendously during that 12 month period of time. In fact, she purchased a new home without my help and was making payments, working as an RN and had a new boyfriend who treated her with respect. I was working the steps, was also changing and developing a spiritual life for the first time. Our relationship improved and we were meeting weekly for lunch sharing our experiences in our respective recovery programs. Things were indeed looking good and then the abusive boyfriend called. He had a severe infection in his foot and convinced my daughter to meet him at his home because he needed her help. He had once again tapped into her caring nature and the relapse process had begun.

During the next two years there was one crisis after another ranging from overdose; suicide attempts, trips to the emergency rooms;

arrests and imprisonment. We were both living in an absolute night-mare but still had a strong faith and spiritual life. She shared the deep shame, guilt and disappointment she felt after each relapse and that she constantly talked to God about her addiction. I had changed my attitude and behavior toward her but still was not able to let her get close to me for fear of getting hurt and disappointed. One thing we both observed during this time was that the general public, including health care professionals, was extremely judgmental and sometimes cruel in their treatment and attitude toward my daughter and me. She told me that this attitude contributed greatly to the shame and guilt she felt. She could not resolve these feelings and instead used crack cocaine and alcohol to relieve them. The consequences after each use were now so severe that she began to give up and could see no way out except suicide. She made six attempts during a two year period.

I had now come to the point where my hope for her recovery was also lost and I became more and more obsessed with the possibility that she would die and that I must continue to try to save her. There was conflict within myself and with the rest of my family about what was enabling behavior versus what was helping her. One of the most difficult things about raising an addicted child is to recognize what is enabling behavior and then to exercise the tough love needed to not engage in it. This is especially difficult in a father and daughter relationship where the father's deepest instincts are to protect and provide comfort. I also felt I was less of a man and a poor father if I could not make things OK for my daughter. The other problem is that after a resolution is made to discontinue a certain enabling behavior, the next crisis is different enough so that the behavior is justified one more time. A combination of guilt and the expectation that this time the outcome will be different drives the decision to "help" one more time. Often when one family member gets into recovery through Al Anon and others do not; disagreements arise about what is helping versus hurting. My family and I were in agreement that we would try to have my daughter committed to a mental health facility. This proved to be difficult but we finally succeeded only to find out two days later that she had been released. The psychiatrist who admitted her said that she could not be held legally against her will for more than 48 hours unless she stated that she intended to end her life. I reminded him of the six documented suicide attempts but it made no difference as his hands were tied by the legal system. This was one of those times when I felt raging anger but there was no target at which it could be effectively directed. Legal precedents overruled common sense and there was nothing I could do about it.

A week later she again used cocaine with the abusive boyfriend and this time he had burned her with a torch and severely cut her arm. She ran to a neighbor's house and was taken to the emergency room and he was finally arrested for deadly assault. She recovered at our home and he was bailed out of jail after 48 hours but faced a felony charge. I had not mentioned this previously but I had been working with the police from the first time this abusive guy harmed her but could do nothing unless she agreed to file charges. There were numerous thoughts and discussions with my sons about taking the matter into our own hands but fortunately we all realized that one or more of us would also end up in prison and make the situation even worse. It was again a situation where the legal process overruled common sense and hard evidence that she was being abused. The fact that he now faced felony charges was a huge relief but the fear remained as long as he was out on bail. During the arrest process, the police confiscated my daughter's purse and then called asking her to pick it up. I drove my daughter to the police station and the officer immediately arrested her for cocaine possession saying they had found 9 grams in her purse. Apparently her boyfriend had placed the cocaine in her purse before the police arrived at his house. I believed this to be true because my daughter would not have tried to retrieve the purse knowing she had cocaine in it. The officer told me she would go to the county jail and remain there until a hearing was scheduled which was to take about two to three weeks. My daughter tearfully begged me to bail her out and I told I could not do that again. I told her that I loved her too much to continue to enable her and that no matter how painful it was for both of us she would need to face these consequences without my help.

Well, my wife and granddaughter were not in agreement on this one. I called them on the way home and before I returned, they had obtained the services of an attorney and started the process to have her bailed out. We argued about this and then learned she had developed a severe infection in her arm from the cut she received from the abusive boyfriend. Knowing that she would not get good medical care in jail, combined with my own doubts about the decision I had made, led me to support my wife and granddaughter in getting her out of jail. She was out in about a week, lived at our home, found a new job and again seemed to be doing OK. Then on Christmas Eve 2005, the horrible phone call came from the coroner's office that she had died of apparent overdose at the boyfriend's home. The feelings at this point are indescribable but seemed like a combination of rage, guilt, extreme sadness and denial that it happened. Guilt was probably the strongest emotion and involved thinking that this was somehow my fault. I deeply regretted not allowing her to get close to me, for judging her, for piling on with lecturing when she relapsed and for not spending more time with her when she was struggling in her early teens. I had to accept that the guilt involved around these behaviors was earned and that it could have contributed to her suffering. About three days after her death, the words "Dad, I'll forgive you if you forgive me" entered my mind. I clearly felt her presence and love and realized that we had forgiven each other for what we each were responsible for and that she was no longer suffering and finally at peace. Despite the addiction she never ceased to love her family and especially her children deeply and we all get to keep that gift from her and use it to love others more.

During the next week or so, we became even more aware of her spirituality and love and that she had positively influenced a lot of people despite the horrors of addiction. We found a note in her apartment listing a number of things she was grateful to God for in her life, we received a number of phone calls from people we did not know saying that she had helped them and a number of people commented that they felt something special at the funeral service. We also became more aware of how much she suffered and how hard she tried to stop the addiction. She had numerous recovery books in her bedroom with notes written in them and had pictures of her son and daughter everywhere.

So is addiction a disease.

Can anything be done about it?

There is absolutely no doubt in my mind that my daughter suffered tremendously with a disease over which she was powerless and which she did not choose to have in her life. How else can one reconcile the difference between the beautiful person she was and the destructive behavior that resulted from her addiction? Not only is addiction a disease, it is also contagious to those who live with or love an addicted person. While the addiction to a substance is not contagious; engaging in irrational, insane behavior is and is also passed on to succeeding generations. If you are reading this book, you probably have an addicted loved one in your life and may still believe that their behavior is willful. If so, you must change this attitude and thinking in order to have any chance of surviving the effects of this disease on YOU.

First, go to an Al-Anon meeting. There you will hear others share their stories, begin to understand that you are not alone and that others have experienced problems much worse than your own. Attend at least six meetings before you decide to abandon the program. By working the program through sharing at meetings, getting a sponsor, working the twelve steps and doing service work you will gradually come to accept addiction as a disease. Once this is done, you will begin to see the addict in a different light and be able to separate the person from the behavior which is caused by the disease. Essentially you will be able to love the person and at the same time hate the disease. You will also begin to see that the addict deeply loves others despite the behavior which seems to indicate otherwise. This change of attitude brings serenity, joy and freedom and many times sobriety to the loved one. They see the changes you have made and want the same for themselves.

Woman's Perspective: Story of Generations of Addiction

Living with addiction everyone becomes overwhelmed, over worked, over stressed, over everything, and evolves into a zombie walking the earth in search of the next problem to conquer, next issue to tackle, the next time the addict indulges too much. Addiction is something that has been passed down from generation to generation seeping its way into lives even before we are born. Though it may not be seen all the time, it still lingers like a shadow in the corner.

Those shadows began in my world before even my own mother was born. It began in a country far away yet it followed my ancestors across the ocean into the land of opportunity. Once prohibition was instituted, my great-grandfather was making "Chock" beer in the basement of his house while 10 plus kids rumbled and romped on the floor above. My own grandfather recalls being told to "cork the bottles" and how when someone drank from a bottle corked by him, that everyone knew he was the one who forced the cork in the bottle for it never had the right fizzing sound once it was unleashed for consumption. Therefore, beer was not only a secret from the law, it was a secret kept within the family for all to participate in; even the youngest of the home were a part of this grand scheme. This is how it begins. With what seems to be normal, yet no one really sees it for what it becomes: addiction.

With the next generation, my grandfather never allowed a drop of any mind-altering substance to touch his lips much less anyone who stepped foot into his home. This policing was dictated to the point to where it was almost an obsession to keep reminding everyone of its evils and that it was a law not to be broken within the walls of his home. Though, much to his trials and efforts, his very own daughter married an alcoholic without her really understanding that the outward signs of addiction were not present but the cancer of the evil lay dormant in her genes only to be accelerated without a conscious effort on her part. Addictions can still merge their way into another life without even realizing its presence by the victim.

Then along came her daughter, one who knew full and well what alcoholism looked like due to the demise of her parent's marriage, she could very clearly see the infection addiction can cause and demolition of a life in the aftermath. Yet, somehow in her quest for moving past all the pain of addiction and abandonment by her father, she stumbles upon a man who genuine in his nature, was being slowly ravaged by addiction. This is my story. This is how it can seemingly be normal for one generation and then seep its way into other generations without much choice. This is where a 12 step program becomes a way of life; to replace; to rebuild and to change the course in subtle, yet powerful ways. This is where life is reclaimed.

Life is reformed after the dust of the rubble is cleared and all that is left are the building blocks of your own life strewn across the dirt. A life that now you own with your actions, your words, your beliefs that a Higher Power has the control over your life. What a relief that can bring to someone in the bowels of living with an addict or loving an addict. That feeling of uselessness will not be a forever curse for you to endure. It becomes the way in which you reemerge as a person of hope. This is the driving force of recovery. This is where life truly begins.

A Special Christmas Letter from a Dad to His Family

By A Fellow Al-Anon

When I received the usual Christmas note this year from Betty, my daughter-in-law, about how "perfect" everything was for their family this past year and about how nice it was to have a loving family like ours; I had a little tingling at the back of my neck. As I thought and prayed about that tingling, I finally identified the source. I had to ask myself this question; is there a widespread denial system in place in our family about addiction? In other words, are we all "sweeping under the rug" what has become commonly known but not spoken since the latest tragic death we have all experienced due to addiction?

The simple truth is that only a year ago we all came together to attend the funeral and mourn the death of John, our oldest son and Betty's brother-in-law, from addiction. That reminded us all that we have people in our family who have problems with drugs, alcohol, depression, ADD, eating disorders, nicotine, etc. It also reminded us that addiction can lead to death! Now Carol and I recently learned that now John's younger brother, Tim, Betty's husband, is admitting that his doctor is telling him that his liver is showing signs of alcoholic liver disease. We were told that Tim tried so hard to do what his doctor told him to do. He drank gallons of water every day in an attempt to clear his liver of the poisons and he even cut back on his drinking!

Now with his doctor reporting some improvement, I can tell you, as a recovering alcoholic myself with over twenty years of sobriety, that Tim interpreted that news as "...I am cured and now I can return to normal drinking"(whatever that is).

Drugs and alcohol have gotten most of my attention during the past twenty years because I have had to work so hard to overcome my own addictions through the 12-Step Programs. Yes, I suffered from ADD as a child back in the days when kids who had trouble focusing were just called lazy. But so much has been learned since those days, and if we really do love each other as much as we say we do in this family, shouldn't we each arm ourselves with as much information as possible about any disease that is harming us?

So how do we help Tim? How do we stop Tim from destroying himself and breaking all of our hearts...again? The tragic truth is this; *we can't!* I have learned the hard way that there is no human power that can stop an alcoholic from taking the next drink. Tim has wondered out loud to me if he can quit, so how on earth could one of us imagine that we could somehow make him quit? Tim is in the grip of a disease that creates a powerful mental and emotional compulsion to drink alcohol. That compulsion renders him incapable of asking for help. And yet, until he does just that, nothing can be done for him!

This brings us squarely to the question; what can we do? First, we can take care to take care of ourselves. This is a family disease and we each have a piece in it. We can seek help from others who have "been there" through community support groups like AA, Nar-A-Non and Al-Anon. I am leading our family by example and have learned *so much* by getting out of Tim's way. I learned this after about two years of attending a men's Al-Anon meeting in our community. I know now that I must allow Tim the dignity of making his own decisions. By learning and growing ourselves we never harm another person. By learning through a program like Al-Anon to detach with love, we can give Tim a fighting chance to reach his own bottom and then reach out for help. Tim needs a family that is recovering alongside him as they cheer him...not a bunch of deniers who continue enabling him while keeping those fake painted smiles on their faces. We need people who give thanks to God every morning that we are still alive; who are big enough to say "but for the grace of God there go I!"

Here are some skills to develop that may help you. These are the combined experience of millions like us who have had to cope with addiction problems in their families.

Do's.

Do learn the facts about alcoholism.

Do talk to someone who understands alcoholism.

Do go to Al-Anon, Alcoholics Anonymous or an alcoholism center.

Do develop an attitude to match the facts.

Do take a personal inventory of yourself.

Do maintain a healthy emotional atmosphere in your home.

Do encourage new activities.

Don'ts

Don't preach or lecture.

Don't argue with a drunk alcoholic.

Don't have a "holier than thou" attitude.

Don't use the "if you loved me" appeal.

Don't make threats you won't carry out.

Don't hide liquor or pour it out.

Don't resent the method of recovery

Don't expect immediate contented sobriety.

Don't try to protect an alcoholic against alcohol.

Don't be discouraged by the mistakes you make.

You may change to word alcohol to drug of choice wherever you wish. A parent never knows how a child will finally come out. When I took my own careful inventory as part of my recovery process I had to look at the example I set for my children. I taught them that alcohol relieved perceived stress. I made alcohol the center of all family get-togethers. I demonstrated that we could not enjoy a meal out or a party without alcohol present. That is how I was taught and I just passed it along to the next generation.

My Dad had terrible depression bouts. He would get so hateful that nobody could stand him. He was never totally incapacitated by his disease but his moods swings had a great deal to do with all of our fears and inability to cope with reality. Don't get me wrong. I do not blame my Dad for my own derelictions but I am aware of how far back this disease goes in our family. The insanity that I am trying to stop with this letter is this; we just keep doing the same things generation after generation while hoping that somehow we will get a different result.

Society accepts now that ADD is caused by a mental/chemical imbalance and some day it is likely to learn the same about alcoholism. People are getting help now for their ADD. Young people throughout our family with ADD are being treated with drugs that help them and those accepting treatment are becoming excellent students. Until we can do the same with addiction shouldn't we do everything we can during this generation to be part of the solution instead of part of the problem?

I am through with living in shame for our family warts. I am tired of sweeping these things under the rug as we continue in lock step to destruction. For this year and for the coming years, let's stop hiding our deficiencies. Let's celebrate that we can now identify them…that we can hold them up to the light and start to correct them! Let's ask God in unison to give us the strength to deal honestly with each other and to seek help when we need it. We have another member of our family who needs help in 2008 but is not capable of asking for it. Let's not allow another tragedy to happen to another loved-one because we all failed to see the problem while failing to support the solution.

I love all of you with my whole heart and soul. I am proud of each of you. You are completely acceptable to me and to my God just as you are but we can all get well. Why don't we get well together…as the family that we are?

Dad.

Epilogue: What is in this for you?

After reading through the book, you may have a few questions about how your life will change if you start a recovery process for yourself. Here we illustrate a few questions that we too asked ourselves and through our own personal recovery found many answers in a 12 Step Program. Not all answers to all questions are here yet many of the first steps in your life of recovery questions are indeed answered below. Thus begins the foundation to a new life in recovery from the affects of someone else's addiction.

So how DO we form healthy working relationships in a marriage with both people working their program? How do you grow mentally, emotionally, physically and spiritually while leading a meaningful life with real purpose? How do you develop the living in the now awareness that means being in constant contact with God...where you see not only the tree but each leaf and sometimes the interesting pattern of the *veins* on the leaf?

Husband's Perspective on Building a New Foundation

When the foundation slab for a house is poured they have to pour the wet concrete over steel cables that are first put under tremendous tension. The tension on the cables, once the concrete hardens, makes an incredibly strong foundation. In a marriage, if one partner offers no resistance, there is no tension and the cables may as well not be there. I take major responsibility for the failures of my early life and of my marriage because I didn't contribute enough tension on my side of the cable. I thought being a good husband was defined as taking care of a dysfunctional wife; being responsible for her economic welfare first and second doing everything that had to be done to keep her happy. That is a perfect formula for an Al-Anon husband. The payoff is that you feel like you are in charge; you appear to be strong in the face of her being weak and pitiful and you get to be the hero because you put up with her.

Every day we each make a profoundly important internal decision. We decide whether to lower our walls…our internal boundaries and receive God's spirit. That is the only real choice. Next we can let in another trusted human being. Now here is my favorite way to do this. My "new" wife (for 27 years as of this writing) and I lower our walls every day. First we sort of "warm up" by doing some spiritual readings at home. We call it "our" meeting. Sometimes for a joke one of us will start with the first few lines of the Al-Anon opening:

"Welcome to the Our Personal Al-Anon meeting. We hope you will find…"

We use a system taught to us by the therapist who helped us merge our families after both of us survived being married to alcoholic spouses and then by the grace of God found each other in Al-Anon. In this system, we are what the therapist called "the executive branch" of the family. After our readings we get out and walk. We believe that angels whisper to us as we walk. It is during these walks that we have our daily board of directors meeting. During these walks we talk about everything. We bounce off of each other on topics large and small; maybe last night's dreams or difficulties we are having in some relationship and often on our own relationship; on our health; on our finances; whatever.

We work with the philosophy in our marriage that we are brother and sister in the eyes of God and, since we are each trying constantly to come closer to God (who is at the top of our marriage) then we cannot help but become closer to each other. This is why we almost every day pray out loud together to our God. A genuine prayer, spoken out loud with my wife does so much. It keeps me real; it keeps me humble; it keeps me honest and it leaves me vulnerable. After that prayer I feel so OK. I am OK with my God and my favorite person on the earth. With this foundation I can go out into the world at ease, knowing that I will not be faced with a situation that God and I together cannot handle.

I would like to revisit the topic that I brought up earlier, this idea of tension in a marriage. Scott Peck, in one of his books, wrote that as a psychiatrist the most diseased marriages he had to treat were marriages where one of the married partners had disappeared. If you do not have tension in your marriage, you probably do not have a strong marriage. So here are some rules that my current wife and I have learned to abide by when the tension gets too high...when we disagree:

1. Never drop the atomic bomb. For anybody with serious abandonment issues, the atomic bomb is **"I'm out-a-here."**

2. Each of us always has the veto power to stop an exchange. Just saying out loud something like "...this is not the best time for me right now. I need some more time to think about this" stops the exchange and puts it on hold until both of us are in a better place emotionally.

3. How important is it? The dog house in a good marriage is not "the big house." Most problems should be relatively small because you have stayed close and open enough on a daily basis that problems big enough to cause a cop to show up at the door with a restraining order were identified long ago.

4. Long lists put me to sleep and I always forget most of the points made, so I will end my list at four. Point number four is this; say out loud that you are not dealing with your enemy here. She is on your side and you are on hers. We are just two humans doing this marriage and humans sometimes say and do things without enough thought. I have had to learn that, just because I thought it an instant ago, doesn't mean that I have to say it out loud to the woman I love!

I would like to finish with an idea. This is a simple device that was taught to me by an author years ago and I still use it. It is a little mnemonic device for remembering how to treat a person we love and it is based on the word **BEST**. This can be applied to any person you love but for the sake of continuity in the book, apply it to the addict woman in your life and see the miracles it can bring forth with time, love, and attention to the details below:

1. **Bless you her. Pray for success in her life, ask God to be with him/her. Always keep her in your prayers.**

2. **Encourage her. If she wants to go back for a Master's Degree, become a cheer leader and pick up some of the slack with the dishes. If she comes in hot from pulling weeds outside go out and look at what she did and thank her for it.**

3. **Secure her. Tell her and show her every hour that she can depend on you to be there for her. Secure her by being present when you are with her.**

4. **And finally; touch her. Most guys want to start with that but there is a reason that it is last. Hug her and kiss her and touch her back when you walk by her in the kitchen.**

In a nutshell, guys, **WORK YOUR PROGRAM**.

Go to your own meetings; keep your insides fresh by constantly pouring out the stale stuff with your sponsor. Work those 12 steps until you know <u>exactly</u> who you are, what you are willing to accept, and what you are NOT willing to accept, and live this program every day, not by yourself, but with the one you love. The diseases of addiction and codependency are causing by far the greatest amount of human loss and suffering. Here is why. Each person is only as free as the sum of their choices. Addiction steals personal freedom. If a codependent alters his thoughts, actions, and words, or stuffs real emotions in an effort to appease or gain "peace at any price", with a confrontational addict, then that person is *also* a victim of the other's addiction. The slavery to the agent has crippled the codependent as well. God meant for all to have free will but how capable are we of exercising it? The inability of the addict to stop choosing the hourly destruction of self...precious self in the form of consciousness, awareness, sentience, thought itself; squanders our greatest gifts. The addicted person squanders memories, knowledge gained, love and their very presence.

At this point you may be asking yourself, "but what about me when I allow the others' addictions to render me less?" We sacrifice great hunks of my self esteem, my options in life, even my future. Every gain that we can make on behalf of mankind between the instant the disease compromises me and my last breath has been damaged by the addictive agent used by another. So please ponder the following points, and then go on your own very real journey of recovery.

1. Whether you realize it at the moment or not, the most important relationship you will ever form is your relationship with your God as you are able to understand God. Your understanding of God will deepen with each successive growth step you make by practicing the Al-Anon program.

2. Your next most important relationship is your relationship with yourself. This relationship affects all the other relation-

ships you have, right down to your every daily experiences, like when there is an encounter with another driver for a few seconds. You look into his or her eyes at an intersection and you both decide who will go first. That was, though brief and temporary, a relationship. But, with the tentacles of addiction reaching out through addiction to all members of the family, much more important relationships are being damaged. Relationships with spouses, children, parents, siblings, and everybody even remotely associated with the family are harmed by addiction. Recovery will recover so many losses, given time.

3. Your own special flavor of spirituality will grow through such habits as attending meetings, being sponsored, and reading Al-Anon literature. Such works as <u>One Day at a Time in Al-Anon</u> and <u>The Courage to Change</u> will provide thoughtful grist on a daily basis.

4. Eventually, when you add a daily prayer with your practice of the eleventh step, your spiritual growth will proliferate into every corner of your life.

5. All program work with other people present, such as attending meetings or spending time with your sponsor, is twelfth-step work! That means you will be contributing to the growth of other people as well as yourself and **that**, my friend, is when your mundane "just going through the motions" existence will become so rich that you can hardly stand it!

6. Not everything in this earthly existence "works" but the principles suggested here have worked for millions of people in 12-Step programs since Bill W. started AA in the late 1930's. As a very wise lady once said during a meeting "…the program is not a fire extinguisher and it is not a Band-Aid. It is a

way of life that works in the long term."

7. On a personal happiness level, as each of the 12 Promises come true. You will just become a happier more effective individual. Even if you have already invested the time and effort to recover and even if you are no longer living with active addiction, when you continue attending the meetings, reading the literature, and working with your sponsor you will continue to become less judgmental; you will learn to care for others and to listen patiently and attentively and you will continue identifying new creative ways to help other people.

On a more global basis, what is to be gained by putting forth the effort to recover from codependency? More years of living and greater quality of life will be gained for any codependent who recovers. However, there are others who stand to gain the same…the addicts whom he or she enables. Our stories are tragedies, yes, and the readers have seen here a rare work that depicts realities; not for the addict but for those nearest the addict. Yet when denial is broken and enabling ends the addict experiences the full impact of his or her addiction. In the words of C.S. Lewis, "Pain is God's megaphone." The addict is more likely to receive God's message when their enabler stops softening the way. In all three of our tales the outcome for the addicted loved-one was horrendous. Slow prolonged deaths, with loss of love, marriages, children, careers, minds, spirits, fortunes, and self-respect…all of this was experienced by the addicts we once loved. With this in mind, we dedicated our work to the daughter who was lost to this disease on the heartrending Christmas Eve in 2005.

Our purpose from the outset was never for financial or personal gain. If our book leads only one codependent enabling man to recovery, then it will be worth our effort to create and promote it. When that man allows his wife, his daughter or his mother or his son or his father or whomever to feel the pain of their disease and stop using, then we will have saved another soul from destruction.

We have the advantage today of looking back to 1986 when Melody Beatty's pivotal work <u>Codependent No More</u> was first published. That work did so much to usher in the entire era of the adult child of the alcoholic. By the time last year's 20-year anniversary issue was released over 4 million copies had been sold. Like her later work, <u>The Language of Letting Go</u>, in all three of our homes are copies of each of Melody Beatty's books. Those books are not gathering dust buried on a shelf. They lie on our night stands. Each is dog-eared, underlined, hi-lighted and marked up because they are still being used as daily readers and/or to serve as sources of great ideas when one of us reviews before leading a meeting.

We will end our book with a description of one morning in the life of a man with years of recovery through the Al-Anon program. Read his description of how the promises of the program have come together to give him a life filled with unimaginable joy, peace, happiness, and meaning. We ask you here; do you want a life that is like his? It is available to you.

Husband's Perspective: What is it like after recovery?

Heard at a meeting: "I hadn't taken a deep breath in about five years!"

I awaken after a good night of sleep that repaired and rested every cell in my body and integrated the memories in my brain from yesterday's experiences. This is the beginning of a high energy morning. But first I enjoy slowly coming to consciousness with that delicious fuzzy warm feeling we all remember when awakening as a child. I take the first three steps in my mind. I begin to share some time with my beautiful, caring, sensitive wife reading spiritual truths out loud to each other in bed followed by a deeply satisfying prayer, which we each speak openly to God, heads on pillows, side-by-side. During our prayers we thank God openly for so many blessings, many of which we list. Then, since we have both spent years practicing the third step, we can easily give over to our God any concern weighing on our hearts.

Neither my wife nor I have to rush to work because we "paid up front." We worked hard and practiced the principles of the Al-Anon program for many years. The various alcoholics and drug addicts who drove us to the program long ago fell to the wayside in various ways while having their adventures but by the grace of God and this program we were both spared having to be dragged down with them. Miracles happened. Our careers were blessed beyond anything either of us could have imagined. We prospered: physically, mentally, financially, relationally and spiritually. Working as a God-centered team, we were able to put four children through college and retire in our early fifties.

I meet a close friend in The Program later and share intellectual, political and spiritual insights...or maybe we talk about last night's game. I know his whole life story and he knows mine. There is mutual respect and trust. We have each told the other personal aspects of our past that not one man in one thousand would share with another.

I go to a noon Al-Anon meeting at the church where four women and two men hug me warmly just because I am me. All six tell me with their eyes and one with words that they love me and they really mean it when they tell me how great it is to see me. I leave the meeting so relaxed....so fulfilled. So much was said by so many on such a deep level that there is a great deal to ponder during my drive home.

I have absolutely no idea what will happen for the rest of the day, but I know that it will be fantastic. I am in the now. I neither regret the past nor deny it but realize that it was all part of God's plan to make me into the man He had in mind in the beginning. The future is really of no concern because I am not in charge of it. The God of the universe is in total charge. I am as natural in my skin as the squirrel I see sitting on a limb in my front yard nibbling on an acorn. We are both God's creatures and everything is going to just fine. All is the way it is meant to be.

I know that my life belongs to God, to my wife, to me and to many others. I know that it is going to be a long, fruitful and interesting one. I have grown spiritually so that I realize that I have many terribly important purposes. I also know that I am capable of completing them and that I am not alone. I have a supporting family, a Program family, close friends and a loving God to cheer for me throughout the process.

Get the picture? That is how I started my day yesterday. It was just a Tuesday.

Woman's Perspective on Emerging as a New Person

No person enters marriage saying they will divorce. For me marriage was a dream laced with the expectation that someone in my life who cares for me will replace or sweep away issues that I experienced in childhood and even adulthood. The problem is that I did not see myself and my role in the demise of the marriage until I had walked into a 12 step meeting and began to work the program. Working the program sent me to the land of getting real with myself and facing me as I was then, now, and in the future. A land that I had avoided for so long for fear that if the real me were to emerge, I would be shredded apart again by addiction of a loved one and my need for dependency upon that loved one. The loved one was at first my ex-husband. When I realized how unfair it was of me to set expectations of a person who himself did not face his demons and hold him responsible for my own happiness was undeniable insanity. To expect him to replace someone who had hurt me in the past meant setting him up for failure and creating the stage within me for the insanity play out. It became a stage production in the life of codependency that was not going to win any awards but become a total disaster from day one. Then I found out exactly what was playing on the stage of my life, codependency.

Once the label of codependency replaced the insanity stage, I was able to accept the fact that my choices had in fact been behind the production of my own life and that no single person was responsible for those choices. They were merely actors in a life gone array who each played their role to get me to the point to where I removed myself from the rubble I had self-created to building a new life on my terms with the help of my Higher Power to guide me with the clarity necessary to keep me within the confines of personal recovery. This allowed me to move beyond my mind controlling everything to finding the balance between thinking, doing, being, and feeling every day. It has given me the clarity to see things just as they are today and not attempt to project what might be or to fester in what was in life. It means here; now, and always with the guide of my Higher Power. Recovering from codependency has brought me into an authentic adulthood. An adulthood that means I am mature due to my experiences, not naïve about what will be from now on, and living as an independent person with compassion. I see situations now with a considered lens that allows to me ensure my own spiritual safety and sanity every day. The lens does not define me but brings about a filter that allows those situations that occur to bounce around in me in a fashion that yields happiness all my own and not dependent upon another to label for me. I can place my own labels upon each situation in my life knowing that I am the one who has chosen the manner in which I allow everyday situations to affect me. I can choose to allow some things into my life and I can choose to disallow other things, people, and situations to happen to me. I am moving from being a completely ego centered codependent to a more balanced soul centered person.

Appendix A: The Twelve Steps of Al-Anon

1. We admitted we were powerless over alcohol...that our lives had become unmanageable.

2. Came to believe that a Power greater than ourselves could restore us to sanity.

3. Made a decision to turn our will and our lives over to the care of God as we understood Him.

4. Made a searching and fearless moral inventory of ourselves.

5. Admitted to God, to ourselves and to another human being the exact nature of our wrongs.

6. Were entirely ready to have God remove all these defects of character.

7. Humbly asked Him to remove our shortcomings.

8. Made a list of all persons we had harmed and became willing to make amends to them all.

9. Made direct amends to such people wherever possible; except when to do so would injure them or others.

10. Continued to take personal inventory and when we were wrong promptly admitted it.

11. Sought through prayer and meditation to improve our conscious contact with God as we understood Him; praying only for knowledge of His will for us and the power to carry that out.

12. Having had a spiritual awakening as the result of these Steps, we tried to carry this message to others and to practice these principles in all our affairs.

Appendix B: How does the medical profession regard AA?

The following description of AA is taken directly from <u>The Merck Manual of Medical Information</u>, second edition, a favorite reference resource for physicians. We chose this definition because is it so accurate but also because it represents a ringing endorsement from a group of highly respected professionals who themselves have spent decades wrestling with the physical deterioration caused by alcoholism.

> *"No approach has benefited so many alcoholics as effectively as the help they can offer themselves by participating in Alcoholics Anonymous. AA is an international fellowship of people who want to stop drinking. There are no dues or fees. The program operates on the basis of the "Twelve steps," which offers the alcoholic a new way of living without alcohol. Members of the fellowship typically work with a sponsor; a fellow member who is abstaining from alcohol use; who offers guidance and support. AA operates within a spiritual context but is not affiliated with any ideology or religious doctrine; however, alternative organizations, such as Life Ring, Recovery (Secular Organizations for Sobriety), exist for those seeking a more secular approach.*
>
> *AA helps its members in other ways as well. It provides a*

place where the recovering alcoholic can socialize away from the tavern with non-drinking friends who are always available for support when the urge to start drinking again becomes strong. In meetings, the alcoholic hears other people relate to the entire group-how they are struggling every day to avoid taking a drink. Finally, by providing a means to help others, AA builds self-esteem and confidence formerly found only in drinking alcohol.

Most metropolitan areas have many AA meetings available day and night, seven days a week. An alcoholic is encouraged to try several different meetings and to attend those at which he feels most comfortable. The Merck Manual of medical Information, 2<u>nd</u> Home Ed., copyright 2003, Pocket Books, p. 651.

Appendix C: The Importance of Connecting AA and Al-Anon

In Praise of Lois and Bill Wilson's Child

In April of 2010 The Hallmark Channel aired a truly pivotal movie titled "When Love Is Not Enough," The Lois Wilson Story. This was a screenplay adapted from the book The Lois Wilson Story written by William G. Bochert. For the first time a major production company put to the screen a realistic picture of what a family member experiences while trying to survive alcoholism in a loved one. Here the world saw an outline of the life story of Lois Wilson, the wife of Bill Wilson, the founder of AA. More importantly, however, from a family member's point of view, it depicted the life story of the person who almost accidentally formed the first 12-step program for the *family members* of alcoholics, Al-Anon.

In this movie, while the opening credits are still on the screen, Winona Ryder, the actress who plays Lois, is doing "voice over" and literally describing the people for whom our book was written. In this dialogue she points out that every alcoholic impacts at least four others, and then she names six others other than herself whose lives were deeply scarred by Bill's drinking: her mother, her father, her younger brother, another married couple with whom both Lois and Bill were close and Eppy Thatcher, the now famous close friend of Bill's who himself had the disease. We rest our case.

A Husband's perspective:
How Important is AA to Al-Anon

I attended the 75th anniversary of AA in July of 2010 in San Antonio, Texas. I joined over 50,000 recovering people to celebrate our mutual recovery. That was the largest convention in the history of San Antonio which is a quintessential "convention city!" During the past 75 years so much has happened. AA has grown to be a major spiritual force for all of mankind and the 12-steps of Alcoholics Anonymous have spawned a bewildering array of programs to help people with every imaginable addiction. In truth, we in Al-Anon owe a huge debt of gratitude to all of those who ever hit a bottom and turned to AA for help (or are at this moment doing so). Both Lois and Bill Wilson lived long enough to see many of the fruits of what they birthed and Lois' spirit was for many of us in attendance in San Antonio as palpable during this five-day celebration as that of Bill's. Al-Anons and "double winners" (i.e. people in both Al-Anon and AA) made up a major portion of the celebrants. Al-Anon meetings alone took up the meeting rooms for entire The Marriot River walk Hotel, where meetings were held in English, Spanish, French, German, and Japanese! But why should family members attend open AA meetings?

Few people realize that the greatest percentage of AA meetings is "open meetings." That means that throughout the week we are blessed by having every day, right in our communities, groups of neighbors who are meeting to help each other outgrow their problems with addiction. These are free, totally anonymous and open to all. We strongly suggest if you are a family member of a person who is either still drinking or recently found recovery that you just show up and learn about this disease first hand. Why?

Here are some sound reasons that we all have for learning about the AA recovery program:

1. You cannot attend an AA meeting without coming away with new-found compassion and respect for those suffering with this disease.

2. Your years of misinformation about alcoholism will dissolve away when you learn the real consequences of alcohol abuse and the real factors that eventually lead an alcoholic deciding to try to get clean and sober.

3. As a family member you will come away with much of your anger and frustration diffused. You will realize that you are not alone; that there really is a way that your loved one can recover; without you even being involved.

4. You will learn that there are more choices for you and your loved ones then you knew even existed before you walked through the door.

5. You will learn that there are no guarantees, even with this, the most successful program for recovery ever designed by man (see praise for AA below from the medical profession).

6. The *"One-Day-At-A-Time"* slogan will have new meaning for you. We all live in our heads, and that is a dangerous neighborhood before recovery. Our heads keep us spinning either in the past or the future, which robs us of the only period of time that is real...the NOW!

7. You will learn the simplest and most comforting truth of all; there is hope.

Survey data about membership in 12 step programs is available only from Al-Anon, as none of the other world service offices gather such data. But recent figures show a disturbing trend. Cooperation, based on the percentage of Al-Anons who were referred to Al-Anon by members of AA, was at an all-time high in 1996 (38%) but in the short nine-year period ending in 2006 that figure had dropped to only 8%. Some guess that this is because people on both sides seem to be regarding meetings held "over there" as "in the enemy camp."

People, this needs to change. I remember with fondness how much the AA people helped me when I first entered recovery in 1976. Here I was, a rare male Al-Anon who was raising three sons who were 10, 13, and 16 while there alcoholic mother was out there on one of her adventures. There was so much love, compassion and just plain time spent with me and my children during meetings and social events held all over town for "all program people." I remember AJ, the wily old ex-marine with over 20 years of sobriety who sort of "adopted" us. AJ spent hours (often during the wee hours of the night) listening patiently to me telling our tales of woe. I remember spaghetti dinners sponsored by AA clubs. I remember the time the AA's sponsored a "roast for Ken" when I had ten years of program and "Fred who lays carpet" stood up and said "...Ken has always been an inspiration to me. I saw Ken when he first came into Al-Anon. He was really a mess! I have always said to myself 'if this guy can get it, I can too!" That kind of left-handed compliment coming from a man with so much sobriety was beyond value for me. It still warms me inside to remember it.

Let me encourage you as a reader right here and now; if you have this disease in your family, it doesn't matter who is swallowing the alcohol or who is enabling the one(s) who are. This is a **family disease** and the program family has to work together to remain a strong part of recovery from it. If we do not then we risk losing everything that Bill and Lois and the millions since them have done to build this world-wide fellowship!

Father's Perspective on How Important AA is to Al-Anon

Since addiction is a family disease, attending open AA meetings with the addicted loved one or alone has a profound impact on an Al-Anon member's recovery. In addition, getting to know other addicts who are in recovery helped me to understand my daughter's disease. Encouraging other family members to attend both AA and Al-Anon meetings is also critical but getting them to attend cannot be controlled.

During my daughter's addiction, I attended open AA meetings with her numerous times. The meeting room has a flyer hanging from the ceiling that says "Miracles Happen Here". After hearing the stories of the addicts and my daughter's story, I began to understand that recovering from the disease of addiction is a miracle and that a spiritual awakening is needed if a miracle is expected.

This spiritual awakening was shown by those who shared at the AA meetings because of their complete honesty, humility and their awareness that they could relapse at any time regardless of whether they had 1 year or 30 years of recovery. They indicated that they are powerless over this disease and that the only hope for recovery is to turn their will and their lives over to God.

Attending these AA meetings made me realize that the disease of addiction is contagious in terms of the emotional impact it has on the entire family. The only difference between the addict and the other family members is that the addict uses a substance. The behaviors resulting from the disease are very similar and the downward spiral until a bottom is hit occurs for both the addict and the family. Attending the AA meetings with my daughter also helped our relationship. After the meetings we shared about our programs, made amends and clearly understood why we behaved the way we did.

My daughter and I also shared about how critical it was for the rest of the family to attend both AA and Al-Anon meetings. We both realized that we cannot control the rest of the family but that we could do the following to encourage them.

1. *Continue attending meetings and working our programs so that we begin to change. This could create a desire for them to attend.*
2. *Invite them ONE TIME to attend a specific meeting with us. Doing this more than once will most likely have a negative result because no one wants to be controlled.*
3. *Make amends to them by completing Step 9. During this discussion, we can point out how the program has given us*

peace and serenity and more importantly how this disease has impacted us in terms of character defects. This could help them to begin thinking about how this disease impacted them and to seek recovery themselves.

4. *After doing the first three things, pray and follow the slogan: Let Go and Let God.*

Addiction is a contagious family disease and like any other family disease, the entire family needs the same treatment. AA and Al-Anon give the same treatment for this disease. I would suggest that after attending Al-Anon and AA meetings that you encourage other Al-Anon members to attend AA meetings and announce the meeting locations and times during your Al-Anon meetings.

Index

References

Al-Anon Family Group Headquarters, Inc. (1975). One day at a time in Al-Anon. New York: Al-Anon Family Group Headquarters, Inc. (Original work published 1973).

Alcoholics Anonymous World Services, Inc. (1976). Alcoholics Anonymous: The story of how many thousands of men and women have recovered from alcoholism (3rd Edition). New York City: Alcoholics Anonymous World Services, Inc. (Original Work published 1939)

As Bill sees it: The A.A. way of life. (1993). New York: Alcoholics Anonymous World Services, Inc. (Original work published 1967).

Courage to change: One day at a time in Al-Anon II. (1992). Virginia Beach, Virginia: Al-Anon Family Group Headquarters, Inc.

Hemfelt, Robert, Dr. & Fowler, Richard, Dr. (1990). Serenity: A companion for twelve step recovery. Nashville, Atlanta, London, Vancouver: Thomas Nelson Publishers.

Frankl, Victor E. (2006). Man's search for meaning. (Ilse Lasch, Trans). Boston: Beacon Press. (Original work published 1959).

Gray, John. Men are from Mars, women are from Venus. (1992). New York: Harper Collins.

Herten, Jeff. An uncommon drunk: Revelations of a high functioning alcoholic. (2006). Lincoln, Nebraska: iUniverse.

Knapp, Caroline. Drinking: A love story. (1996). New York: Dial Press.

Meeker, Meg. Strong fathers, strong daughters: 10 secrets every father should know. (2007). New York: Ballantine Press.

Merck Manual (14th Ed.) (1982). Rathway, New Jersey: Merck Sharp & Dohme Research Laboratories.

Reid, Fiona A. (2006). Mammals of North America (Rev. ed.). New York: Houghton Mifflin Company.

Wegscheider, Sharon. (1981). Another chance: Hope and health for the alcoholic family. Palo Alto, California: Science and Behavior Books, Inc.